MINI

ENCYCLOPEDIA

ROCKS
& FOSSILS

ROCKS
& FOSSILS

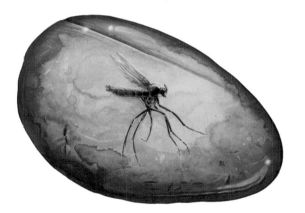

Authors
Chris and Helen Pellant

Consultants
Keith Ambrose, Steve Parker, and Clint Twist

Miles
Kelly

First published as *Rocks & Fossils* in 2010 by Miles Kelly Publishing Ltd
Harding's Barn, Bardfield End Green, Thaxted, Essex, CM6 3PX, UK

This edition printed 05/14

LOT#:
2 4 6 8 10 9 7 5 3 1

Publishing Director Belinda Gallagher
Creative Director Jo Cowan
Cover Designer Jo Cowan
Series Designer Helen Bracey
Volume Designer Martin Lampon (Tiger Media Ltd)
Junior Designer Kayleigh Allen
Image Manager Liberty Newton
Indexer Gill Lee
Production Manager Elizabeth Collins
Reprographics Stephan Davis, Jennifer Cozens
Assets Lorraine King
Contributers Steve Parker, Clint Twist

ISBN 978-1-4351-5643-2

Printed in China

British Library Cataloguing-in-Publication Data
A catalogue record for this book is available from the British Library

Made with paper from a sustainable forest

www.mileskelly.net
info@mileskelly.net

Contents

 Rocks

Minerals

Fossils

Rocks

What is a rock?

A rock is an aggregate (mixture) of mineral particles. It may be made of loose sand (sandstone) or sticky clay (mudstone), fossil and fossil debris (limestone) or mineral crystals welded together (igneous and high grade metamorphic rocks).

Scientists classify rocks into three main groups—igneous, sedimentary, and metamorphic.

Rocks began to form as soon as the original molten (liquid) Earth started to cool around 4,000 mya.

The first rocks to form were igneous rocks. These crystallized from molten magma (underground) or lava (on the surface).

Rocks form in a cycle. Igneous rocks are weathered and eroded and formed into sedimentary rocks. These may be altered by metamorphism (the effect of extreme heat or pressure) and eventually, if they are buried very deep in the Earth's crust, they melt and become igneous rocks again.

The age of rocks can be worked out by studying the fossils they contain or the breakdown of radioactive elements contained in them. This is called radiometric dating.

DID YOU KNOW?
The oldest rocks to be radiometrically dated are more than 3,900 million years old.

As soon as the Earth's atmosphere had begun to develop, around 2,000 mya, weathering and erosion began to break down the early igneous rocks to make sediments.

◈ **Metamorphic rocks** are created when earlier-formed rocks are changed by heat from magma or lava or by pressure and heat deep underground.

◈ **Rocks are being formed** all the time. The mud and sand on the beach or in a riverbed may become a sedimentary rock.

▼ *Igneous, metamorphic, and sedimentary rocks are repeatedly changed into each other, on the Earth's surface and underground. They can all become any of the other types of rock.*

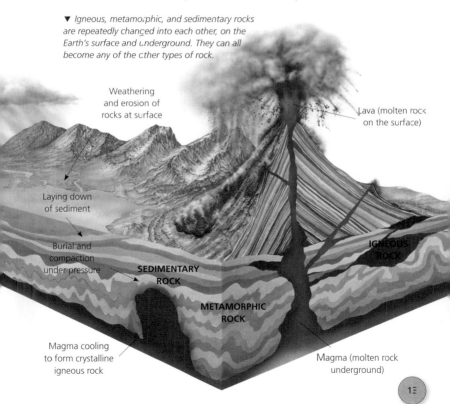

Weathering
and erosion of
rocks at surface

Lava (molten rock
on the surface)

Laying down
of sediment

Burial and
compaction
under pressure

**SEDIMENTARY
ROCK**

**IGNEOUS
ROCK**

**METAMORPHIC
ROCK**

Magma cooling
to form crystalline
igneous rock

Magma (molten rock
underground)

13

What are igneous rocks?

▲ In a thin slice of granite magnified many times, the crystals are clearly seen. The gray crystals are quartz and feldspar and the brighter colors are mica.

◀ **Geologists** sometimes call igneous rocks primary rocks because they form from molten material that originates deep in the Earth's crust.

◀ **Igneous rocks** can be distinguished from other rocks because they are made of a mosaic of mineral crystals, usually without layers.

◀ **The crystals** in igneous rocks are usually welded together.

◀ **Igneous rocks** occur in many different structures, both underground (intrusive) and on the surface (extrusive).

◀ **Intrusive igneous rocks** form underground in large masses called batholiths, and relatively small intrusions, for example, sills and dikes.

◀ **Extrusive igneous rocks** build volcanoes. These may have large rocky craters or be mountains of ash and dust.

- **Igneous rocks** are the best rocks for radiometric dating because the crystals in them formed at a definite time in the past. These crystals may not have altered since their formation, so an accurate date can often be obtained. Radiometric dating is most accurate if the rocks used are fresh and unweathered.

- **Basalt** is a volcanic igneous rock that makes up more of the Earth's crust than any other rock. It covers the vast ocean basins.

- **Granite**, an intrusive igneous rock that forms deep underground, makes up much of the Earth's continental crust.

- **Some igneous rocks**, such as granite and dolerite, are very hard and durable and are quarried for use in road surfaces.

▼ *Crater Lake in Oregon is the remains of a collapsed volcano called a caldera. The small cone forms Wizard Island.*

Granite

One of the best-known igneous rocks is granite due to its colorful crystalline appearance. Polished slabs are used to decorate buildings.

It is a coarse-grained igneous rock with crystals that are easily seen by the naked eye. They are generally more than 5 mm across. Granite also contains white or pink crystals of feldspar and black or silvery white mica.

Other minerals found in granite, which don't affect its classification, are called accessory minerals. These include pyrite, tourmaline, and apatite.

▼ *This granite on the Isle of Mull, western Scotland, UK, has been weathered along its vertical joints. The pink color results from large amounts of feldspar in the rock.*

◄ *The sport of curling uses granite stones. Teams slide large, heavy, polished granite disks along the ice toward a target.*

Granite contains a large amount of quartz. This common mineral is off-white or gray, greasy-looking, and very hard.

Granite forms deep in the Earth's crust in large chambers of molten magma called batholiths. The magma cools very slowly, often taking many millions of years, which enables the crystals in granite to grow to a large size.

For granite to be exposed at the surface, many thousands of feet of rock have to be weathered and eroded. Rocks may also be pushed up by mountain building processes before granite is exposed on the Earth's surface.

Granite is not as hard and durable as many people think. It is easily weathered, especially in humid climates, and decomposes to sand and clay.

In the area around a mass of granite, there is a region of metamorphism where heat from the magma has changed the original rocks.

In the area near to a granite batholith it may be possible to mine for tin, copper, lead, zinc, and other minerals.

Batholiths

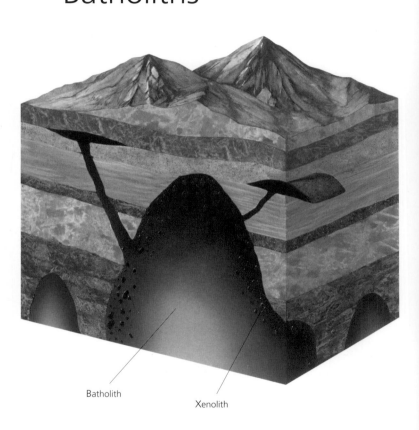

Batholith

Xenolith

▲ *A batholith is a gigantic mass of magma formed deep below a mountain range. Small offshoots of magma may rise from it higher into the Earth's crust. Lumps of rock called xenoliths may be present in the batholith.*

- **A batholith** is a very large mass of igneous rock that was originally magma.

- **Batholiths** are commonly formed deep in the roots of mountain chains and may be many tens of miles in diameter.

DID YOU KNOW?

The giant batholith in the Andes Mountains of Peru covers an area 995 mi by 120 mi.

- **In Britain**, a batholith exists under much of Cornwall, England, and reaches out under the sea to the Scilly Isles. This covers an area of 40 mi by 25 mi. Many batholiths are larger than this.

- **Before the giant mass** of magma in the batholith was intruded (forced in), there was other rock in that part of the Earth's crust. Geologists have puzzled over what happened to the original rock. It is believed that some of it was melted and incorporated into the magma.

- **Granite magma** itself may be the result of the melting of other rock at great depth.

- **Sills and dikes** may stretch upward from some batholiths.

- **Most batholiths** are made of granite. Some contain other coarse-grained igneous rocks such as syenite and gabbro.

- **Even when the rock** in a batholith has been crystalline for millions of years, heat will still rise through it from a great depth. This heat may be trapped if clay and other rock have formed later.

- **Scientists** have discovered that this heat could be used to produce electricity in a safe, clean way.

Granodiorite

- **One of the most common** igneous rocks is granodiorite.

- **As its name suggests**, this rock has some features of the acidic granites and some features of the intermediate rocks.

- **Granodiorite is an attractive**, coarse-grained rock. The crystals making up the mass of the rock can easily be seen with the naked eye.

- **The main minerals** in granodiorite are feldspar, quartz, hornblende, augite, and mica.

- **There are two main color varieties** of granodiorite. One is pink because of the color of most of the feldspar in the rock. White granodiorite contains pale-colored feldspar.

- **This rock looks** similar to granite. When its minerals are examined and the total silica content worked out, it can be seen that it is an intermediate, not an acid rock.

DID YOU KNOW?

Much of the so-called "granite" used as a decorative polished rock is actually granodiorite.

- **In many types of igneous intrusions**, granodiorite can be found, especially those formed at some depth below the surface of the Earth.

- **When this rock occurs** in large intrusions, it is often associated with granite.

▲ *This attractive rock is colored by its minerals. The pink mineral is feldspar, dark colors are hornblende and biotite mica, and the pale mineral is quartz.*

The vast batholith in southern California covers a surface area of more than 3,000 sq mi. Much of it is made of granodiorite.

Because of its coloring and crystalline appearance, granodiorite is used for ornamental purposes.

Gabbro

◀ **A dark igneous rock**, gabbro is made of quite large crystals and has a speckled appearance.

◀ **Gabbro** forms as large masses of magma cool, as granite does, but it is made of different minerals. Because it cools slowly, it has large, easily visible crystals.

◀ **Rather than occurring** in batholiths, gabbro is commonly found in thick sheets of igneous rock.

◀ **Feldspar and pyroxene** are the two main minerals in gabbro, but it also has a small amount of quartz—less than 10 percent.

◀ **Feldspar is a pale mineral**, often occurring in thin crystals in gabbro, while pyroxene is almost black, giving the rock its speckled appearance.

▼ *The jagged gabbro peaks of the Cuillins seen across Loch Slapin on the Isle of Skye, UK.*

▶ *Gabbro is a dark-colored rock with a black-and-white speckled appearance.*

🔖 **Compared with granite**, gabbro is a very dark-colored rock, and is also noticeably heavier. This is because it contains a large amount of pyroxene, which is a dense mineral.

🔖 **A mineral called olivine** is sometimes found in gabbro. This is a green or brownish mineral rich in iron and magnesium, which crystallizes at very high temperatures.

🔖 **Gabbro** mainly forms in the Earth's crust beneath the basalts of the ocean floors but can also occur on continents. Granite typically occurs in a continental setting.

🔖 **Some famous masses** of gabbro are at Bushveldt in South Africa and Stillwater, Montana.

🔖 **In Britain**, the Cuillin Hills on the Isle of Skye, in western Scotland, are largely made of gabbro, which weathers into jagged peaks.

Pegmatite

Pegmatite is an igneous rock formed deep underground and made up of very large crystals. These may be more than one inch long. In some pegmatite rocks, giant crystals over 3 ft long have been discovered.

For such large crystals to form, the magma must cool very slowly, allowing the crystals a long time to develop.

Pegmatite occurs in sheets and other structures, often around the margins of large scale intrusions.

Sills and dikes of pegmatite also occur in many areas of very old gneiss.

Usually, pegmatite has a similar composition to granite, containing mainly feldspar, mica, and quartz. However, gabbro and syenite pegmatites are not unknown.

Pegmatite generally crystallizes from magma and other high-temperature fluids, which are rich in many rare elements. These include niobium, tantalum, lithium, and tungsten. This makes some pegmatites economically valuable.

Among the extra minerals that are often found in pegmatites are tourmaline, topaz, fluorite, apatite, and cassiterite.

Radioactive elements, such as autunite and torbernite, also occur in pegmatite.

Some pegmatites have an attractive appearance called graphic texture. This looks rather like ancient writing and is created by quartz and feldspar crystals merging in the rock.

▼ This intrusion of pegmatite is full of large, pink feldspar crystals. It has cut into dark-colored metamorphic rock.

Porphyry

🔹 **Rocks of medium grain size** that contain large crystals set into the finer ground mass are referred to as porphyry.

🔹 **These rocks have formed** in minor intrusions, such as sills and dikes.

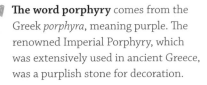

🔹 **The word porphyry** comes from the Greek *porphyra*, meaning purple. The renowned Imperial Porphyry, which was extensively used in ancient Greece, was a purplish stone for decoration.

🔹 **Porphyry is still used** as an ornamental stone today.

🔹 **The name porphyry** is often used in combination with a mineral name, such as quartz porphyry.

🔹 **The large crystals in porphyry** are usually feldspars, but may be quartz or other minerals.

◀ *The Portrait of the Four Tetrarchs sculpture was made of porphyry.*

▲ *Large feldspar and other crystals set in a fine-grained, dark matrix give this andesite, from Scandinavia, a porphyritic texture.*

- **The formation of porphyry** is closely related to the way in which magma, from which the rock is made, has cooled.

- **Molten rock found deep in the Earth's crust** is called magma. When it rises, it cools, and minerals then crystallize. The magma around the first crystals to form is still liquid and mobile.

- **Magma containing solid crystals** may rise into a fracture in the crust and form a dike. The mass of rock will cool rapidly around the previously formed crystals, making porphyry.

- **A striking form** of porphyry, from Scandinavia, contains large, diamond-shaped crystals, and is called rhomb porphyry.

Xenoliths

▼ Large, dark xenoliths can be easily seen in this eroded mass of igneous diorite. They were surrounded by molten magma and partly changed by its heat.

- The word **"xenolith"** comes from the Greek *xenos*, which means "stranger" and *lithos*, meaning "stone."

- These **"stranger stones"** are found around the margins of many igneous intrusions, where magma has melted and forced its way into other rocks. They may also be found in lava.

- They are **lumps of rock** that have been broken off and engulfed by the igneous rock, so are strangers in their new location.

- **Xenoliths** often appear as dark, rounded or irregular rocks set into granite or another igneous rock.

- **Near the very edge** of the igneous intrusion, a xenolith will not have been heated too much by the magma and so keeps many of its original features.

- **Xenoliths** found some feet into the igneous rock will have been altered considerably and metamorphosed. They may even have crystals in them similar to those in the igneous rock.

- **Xenoliths** help geologists to work out the types of rock the magma passed through as it was being intruded or erupted.

- **In some places** blocks of the very lowest crustal rocks have been brought to the surface by rising magma. These xenoliths allow geologists to study rocks not normally seen on the surface.

- **In the diamond-bearing rocks** around Kimberly, South Africa, xenoliths that may be derived from the Earth's mantle (the region beneath the crust) are found.

- **Large amounts of xenolith rock** caught up in magma may react with it and change its composition.

Syenite

Syenite is an intrusive igneous rock that has formed by the cooling of magma deep in the Earth's crust.

Because of the slow cooling associated with the high temperatures at great depth, syenite has large crystals and is a coarse-grained rock. The crystals can be seen with the naked eye.

Syenite may look rather like granite, but by studying the minerals it contains, differences can be seen.

Syenite will usually appear darker-colored than granite, but not as dark as gabbro. Some syenites may be pink or gray or tinged with violet.

One well-known type of syenite is called larvikite. It is from Norway and is commonly cut into slabs and polished to make a pearly blue-green ornamental stone. This has been used as a facing stone on many buildings throughout the UK.

◄ The syenite that is found mainly around Oslo in Norway is called larvikite. This rock is dark-colored and prized for its bluish iridescence.

- **As well as occurring** in large intrusions, syenite is also found in sills and dikes. These rocks tend to have smaller crystals.

- **Many syenites** have large crystals set into a finer mass, giving an attractive appearance. This is called a porphyritic texture.

- **As well as feldspar and quartz**, syenite can contain hornblende, pyroxene, and the dark mica biotite. This composition contains features of both granite and gabbro.

- **Microsyenite** is an igneous rock with the composition of syenite, but contains smaller crystals.

- **Rhomb porphyry** is a type of microsyenite found commonly in Norway. Pebbles of it, which have been carried by ice sheets across the North Sea area, are often found on the east coast of England.

▼ *When polished for ornamental use, the bluish iridescence of the feldspar crystals in larvikite can easily be seen.*

Dikes and sills

🔹 **Dikes and sills** are called minor igneous intrusions because they are of moderate to small size.

🔹 **Both intrusions** are sheets of igneous rock and are commonly made of rocks such as dolerite that have cooled quite quickly and are fine-grained.

🔹 **They are usually measured** in meters, being anything from one or 2 m in thickness to a few hundred.

🔹 **A dike** is very often a vertical sheet of dark rock cutting across existing strata (layers). Geologists call this a discordant intrusion.

🔹 **The magma** forming the dike will have risen into a fracture in the overlying rocks.

🔹 **Dikes are often found** in great numbers, or swarms. One such swarm occurs in the Inner Hebrides across southern Scotland and stretches into the north of England, UK.

🔹 **A sill**, in contrast, follows the rock structures in the area where it is intruded. This is called a concordant intrusion. In sedimentary rocks, they are generally intruded along bedding planes.

DID YOU KNOW?
On the Isle of Arran, Scotland, UK, 525 dikes occur within a distance of 15 mi. These have stretched the Earth's crust by 7 percent.

🔹 **Because they are small** structures giving out little heat, there is usually only a small metamorphic effect on neighboring rocks.

🔹 **Like many lava flows**, sills may form vertical columns of rock that result from the way the magma has cooled. This is known as columnar jointing.

Sedimentary strata   Volcano   Dike   Sill

Magma

▲ Dikes and sills are both small igneous intrusions. Dikes cut across the strata and sills follow the existing layers of rock.

Dolerite

🔹 **Dolerite** is a dark-colored igneous rock, often with an overall speckled appearance.

🔹 **The speckled surface** results from the minerals it contains. These are light-colored feldspar and black pyroxene. There is also a small amount of pale-gray quartz. This is the same composition as gabbro and basalt.

🔹 **Dolerite** may contain the green or brownish mineral called olivine.

🔹 **It is possible** to see its crystals with the naked eye, but to study them in detail a strong hand lens is needed. Geologists refer to this type of rock as being medium-grained.

🔹 **Dolerite** commonly occurs in small igneous intrusions, such as sills and dikes, where magma has cooled much more rapidly than in a batholith.

▼ *Dolerite is a hard igneous rock used mainly for road stone. Its vertical columnar structure can be seen in the quarry faces.*

▲ *The Vorontsovsky Palace was built in modern-day Crimea, between 1830 and 1848. It is constructed mainly of locally quarried dolerite.*

Rounded vertical masses of dolerite may be the necks of old volcanoes. These remain after the lava and ash of the volcano have been eroded.

Dolerite-forming magma originates very low in the Earth's crust or in the upper mantle. The rock is generally associated with thin oceanic crust rather than areas of thick continental crust.

Dolerite is a dense, heavy rock mainly because it contains minerals that are rich in iron.

American geologists use the term diabase for this type of rock.

Dolerite is a very hard and durable rock. It is extensively quarried for road stone, railway ballast, and other uses.

Serpentinite

◆ **Serpentinite** is unlike many igneous rocks in a number of vital ways. It is thought to be formed by the chemical alteration of other igneous rocks.

◆ **It often contains** very attractive colors, such as shades of green and red. These colors often make veins through the rock.

◆ **Because it is easily cut**, shaped, and polished, serpentinite is often used ornamentally. This is especially true in areas where it is a common rock, such as around the Lizard Peninsula in Cornwall, UK.

▲ *The Inuit travel for days to reach supplies of serpentinite, which they carve into beautiful shapes.*

◆ **Serpentinite** is made largely of a variety of "serpentine" minerals. These include chrysotile and antigorite, which are both silicate minerals with a slippery, soapy feel and fibrous structure.

◆ **Chrysotile** is a source of asbestos, once used for its insulating properties.

◆ **Serpentinites** contain virtually no quartz, but can contain a number of silicate minerals, such as garnet, mica, hornblende, and pyroxene.

- **It is generally believed** that serpentinites were originally dense, heavy rocks related to the lowest parts of the Earth's crust. These were rich in minerals such as olivine, and have been much altered by the addition of water.

- **In some examples**, there is little indication as to what the original rock may have been because the serpentinization is so extreme.

- **Serpentinites** are found in many areas including Cornwall, Anglesey, and Shetland, UK, New Zealand, New South Wales, Australia, and Montana.

- **Serpentine minerals** are also found in a group of meteorites called carbonacecus chondrites.

▼ *The coast of the Lizard Peninsula in Cornwall, UK, where serpentinite occurs.*

Volcanoes

🔺 **A volcano** is an opening in the Earth's crust through which lava escapes.

🔺 **Depending on the type** of lava and other volcanic materials, the volcano may be a low, gently sloping structure or a steep, cone-shaped mountain.

🔺 **Some volcanoes** have a single opening. These are called central volcanoes. Others have a number of vents and are called fissure volcanoes.

🔺 **Volcanoes** from which basalt lava erupts are not as violent as those that produce rhyolite and andesite lavas. Basaltic lava has a higher temperature and a less sticky silica than rhyolite and andesite lavas. This means that it flows easily away from the vent.

🔺 **The Hawaiian**, or shield, volcanoes are made of basalt. They have large craters and low domes that spread many tens of miles. The base of Mauna Loa in Hawaii is 70 mi in diameter.

🔺 **Strombolian volcanoes**, named after the island of Stromboli to the north of Sicily, are classic cone shapes. Eruptions can be violent. As well as lava there are layers of ash and dust.

🔺 **Vesuvian volcanoes**, named after Mount Vesuvius in Italy, erupt only once every ten or more years. The lava is sticky and plugs the vent, causing violent eruptions.

DID YOU KNOW?
Mauna Loa in Hawaii is the world's largest active volcano. From the seabed it is more than 30,000 ft high.

▶ Lava, ash, rock fragments, and gas erupt from this volcano. The cone is built up of layers of lava and ash.

Dust and gas cloud

Pelean volcanoes, named after Mount Pelee in Martinique, are among the most violent. These erupt sticky, silica-rich lava, which often solidifies in the volcano. A great pressure then builds up as more lava tries to get through, and much of the volcano is blown apart by the eruption.

Volcanoes can be very destructive. In 1883, Krakatoa in Java erupted, sending a huge dust cloud around the Earth's atmosphere. This affected the climate for three years. Over 36,000 people died as a result of the eruption.

Volcanic bomb

Layers of lava ash

Volcanic pipe

39

Where volcanoes occur

🔹 **The distribution of volcanoes** is closely linked to lines of weakness in the Earth's crust and its varying thickness.

🔹 **In ocean areas**, the crust is less than 6 mi thick, but below the great continents it may be 40 mi thick. Lava can escape more easily to the surface where the crust is thin.

🔹 **The Earth's crust** and the uppermost part of the underlying layer, the mantle, make up the lithosphere. This is divided into a number of plates.

▼ *Most active volcanoes occur along the "Ring of Fire" (colored red).*

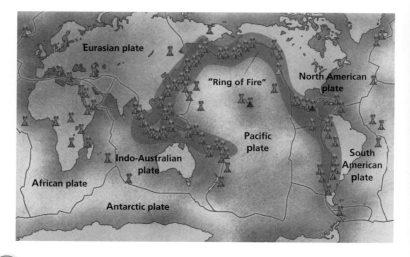

- **The lithospheric plates** are internally solid but constantly move. Some collide, others move away from each other. It is along these plate boundaries that volcanic activity is concentrated.

- **The "Ring of Fire"** around the Pacific Ocean has been studied for many years as many of the world's volcanoes are located in this region. The Pacific Ocean floor is the largest of Earth's plates and around its edges are weaknesses where erupting basaltic lavas can well up to the surface.

- **The volcanoes** in Southeast Asia, Japan, and South and North America are all part of the Ring of Fire.

- **In the Atlantic**, the situation is different. There are two major plates making up this ocean basin, which are moving away from each other. The Mid-Atlantic Ridge, which is mainly below sea level, is a line of active volcanoes.

- **In Iceland**, the Mid-Atlantic Ridge reaches above sea level. This large island is made almost entirely of volcanic rock.

- **There are other regions** where eruptions are caused by plates moving apart from each other. The African Rift Valley is one place where this process is beginning—volcanoes such as Kilimanjaro occur.

- **The Hawaiian volcanoes** are in the center of the Pacific plate, forming a chain of islands. They lie above a plume of hot material rising from the base of the crust.

Basalt

🔹 **There is more basalt** in the Earth's crust than any other rock. Beneath a thin layer of sediment, it covers the ocean floor. More than 90 percent of the volcanic rocks on the Earth are basalt.

🔹 **Basalt** is a volcanic rock that often erupts nonviolently and can flow great distances.

🔹 **It is a dark-colored rock** and its crystals can rarely be seen on its surface without a microscope. Basalt is what geologists call a fine-grained rock.

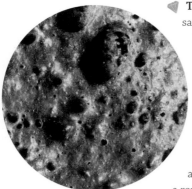

▲ This specimen of basalt from Hawaii is full of vesicles. These are small holes made by gas bubbles in the molten lava.

🔹 **The composition** of basalt is the same as that of gabbro and dolerite. It contains small crystals of feldspar, pyroxene, and common olivine with a small amount of quartz.

🔹 **When it erupts**, basalt lava contains much gas. As the rock cools, gas-bubble hollows are left in the solid rock. These are called vesicles, and give the rock a rough texture.

🔹 **Many fine mineral specimens**, including agate, develop in the vesicles, often long after the rock has cooled.

🔹 **Basalt** is a dense, heavy rock. It contains iron-rich minerals, which because of their magnetism, have been of great use in working out the movement of the Earth's plates.

Basalt lava flows often develop amazingly regular six-sided columns when cool. The Giant's Causeway in Northern Ireland, UK, is a fine example of this feature.

Rocks recovered from the Moon are basaltic. These contain very similar minerals to those found in terrestrial basalts.

▼ *The flow lines can be clearly seen on the surface of this basalt in Iceland.*

Andesite

🔹 **The rock andesite** is solidified from a type of lava that erupts from violent volcanoes.

🔹 **The name of this rock** is taken from the Andes Mountains in South America, where much of the rock occurs.

▼ *The crater of Poas, Costa Rica, is filled with a pool of highly acidic water. Layers of andesitic ash and lava can be seen around the crater rim.*

- **Andesite is a fine-grained rock**. The individual crystals making the body of the rock (its matrix) cannot be seen in detail with the naked eye.

- **This type of lava** is referred to by geologists as an intermediate igneous rock. It is between basalt and rhyolite in its chemical composition.

- **The main minerals in** andesite are plagioclase feldspar, pyroxene, amphibole, biotite, and mica.

- **This rock has a medium** to dark color. It is not as dark as basalt, nor as pale in color as rhyolite.

- **Some andesite lavas** are so rich in gas that when they solidify into rock, the rock is filled with gas cavities called vesicles.

- **Large crystals, a few inches in length**, occur in some andesites. These formed before the lava erupted. Such rocks are said to have a porphyritic texture.

> **DID YOU KNOW?**
> Andesite volcanoes erupt large amounts of dust and ash. The devastating eruption of Krakatoa in 1883 produced millions of tons of andesite lava. Its eruption could be heard nearly 3,000 mi away.

Rhyolite

🔹 **This hard, flinty rock** is formed by the solidifying of lava.

🔹 **This rock contains** a high proportion of silica, which means the lava from which rhyolite forms is classified by geologists as acidic lava.

🔹 **As acid lavas** contain more than 65 percent silica they are viscous (sticky).

🔹 **The volcanoes from which rhyolitic lava** is erupted are extremely violent. This is because the viscous lava doesn't flow far, and may block the vent as it cools, leading to a build-up of pressure.

◄ Rhyolite volcanoes are explosive and very violent when they erupt.

▶ *The thin lines in this close-up specimen of rhyolite are called flow-banding. They were caused when molten lava flowed from the volcano.*

◀ **Some acidic lava volcanoes** develop a tall spine of solidified rhyolite lava above the cone.

◀ **Rhyolite is generally a pale-colored rock**, paler than basalt or andesite.

◀ **The minerals in rhyolite** are too small to be seen without a hand lens or microscope. This is because it has solidified quickly.

DID YOU KNOW?

Because it is hard, and may break with a sharp fracture, rhyolite was used for making tools and axes during Neolithic times.

◀ **Rhyolite contains high proportions** of quartz and feldspar. These minerals are often glassy, as they have cooled so rapidly. Mica may also occur.

◀ **A banded structure**, often seen in rhyolite, results from the flow of the molten rock.

Rock columns

In many parts of the world there are famous igneous rock formations where the rock is in almost perfect vertical columns. These include The Giant's Causeway (Antrim, Northern Ireland, UK), Waikato Dam, (North Island, New Zealand), and Svartifoss waterfall (Iceland).

The columns may be many tens of feet high and can be perfectly symmetrical and usually six-sided.

The igneous rock involved is very often basalt, although dolerite, rhyolite, and welded tuff may also form columns.

Columnar structures are seen best in lava flows, but they also form less perfectly in sills.

Sills and lava flows have vertical columns as they cool from the base and top. In a dike, columns may develop horizontally as the rock cools from its vertical edges.

▼ The Giant's Causeway in Northern Ireland, UK, is made of thousands of interlocking basalt columns.

▲ *The vertical columns on the Isle of Staffa, Scotland, UK, have a mass of uneven lava above them. The dark opening is Fingal's Cave.*

When a lake or pond dries out, the wet mud on its bed shrinks into a pattern of polygonal cracks. Igneous rocks behave like this but in a more regular way.

The processes that allow such regular shapes to form in cooling rock probably involve contraction and an even loss of heat throughout the rock.

As a lava flow ceases to move, it begins to cool and form solid igneous rock. The base cools regularly and contraction begins to occur. Cracks develop and columns grow up through the lava.

Columnar formations usually have a more perfect lower part and a less regular shape toward the top.

A hexagonal shape allows the columns to fit together perfectly, but there can be columns with three to eight sides.

49

Geothermal springs

- **In many areas** where volcanic activity takes place (or has recently occurred), there are hot springs, or geysers.

- **The word "geyser"** comes from the Icelandic *geysir*, meaning a "spouter" or "gusher." In Iceland, there are a number of regions where heated underground water gushes to the surface.

- **Hot water** from underground is used in Iceland for central heating and heating greenhouses in which fruit, vegetables, and even bananas are grown.

- **In many regions**—such as California, Weiraki, New Zealand, and Larderello, Italy—projects have been established to try to generate electricity from underground steam.

- **An individual geyser** consists of a central pipe with many branches leading from it at depth. Water heated volcanically underground becomes pressurized. As the mass of water boils, it bursts vertically through the central pipe and into the air. Some geysers erupt 230 ft into the air.

◀ Strokkur *(Icelandic for "churn")* is a geyser in Iceland. It erupts regularly, every 5–10 minutes, and can shoot water up to 80 ft into the air.

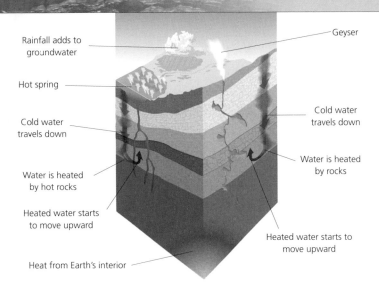

Rainfall adds to groundwater

Geyser

Hot spring

Cold water travels down

Cold water travels down

Water is heated by rocks

Water is heated by hot rocks

Heated water starts to move upward

Heated water starts to move upward

Heat from Earth's interior

▲ When rainwater seeps into the earth, it can be heated by hot rocks underground before rising back up to the surface as hot springs, pools, and geysers.

🔹 **A number of geysers** are very regular in their spouting, and they remain constant over many years.

🔹 **On the surface**, a geyser is surrounded by a pool of silica-rich water at a temperature of about 185°F. Deposited in this and around its margins is a silica rock called geyserite, which makes a mound around the opening.

🔹 **A fragment of wood** taken from the geyserite surrounding the Old Faithful Geyser in Yellowstone National Park has been dated at 730 years old. This suggests how long that geyser has been spouting.

What are sedimentary rocks?

🔹 **Sedimentary rocks** are best recognized by their layers. These bedding planes, or strata, result from the way the sediment has been deposited.

🔹 **These rocks** are formed in a wide variety of environments on the Earth's surface, and in many cases are easier to study than igneous rocks, which often form at great depth in the Earth's crust.

🔹 **Many sedimentary rocks** are made of particles that have been eroded or weathered from pre-existing rocks. For this reason, they are often referred to as secondary rocks.

▲ *Sandstone is light in color and made mainly of sand.*

🔹 **The particles** are transported by rivers, wind, glaciers, and gravity. During this journey they are changed and may become smaller, more rounded, and broken.

🔹 **Eventually**, when the transporting medium is no longer able to carry the sediment particles, they are deposited. A river, for example, can only carry large pebbles when it is flowing swiftly. As it slows down, this material is left behind.

🔹 **Most sedimentary rocks** are formed on the seabed. A river entering the sea slows down, depositing its load. The continental shelves have a great thickness of sediment, but much also reaches deeper parts of the oceans.

- **Sedimentary rocks** are of great importance. By looking at their detailed features and comparing these with how modern sediments are being formed, geologists can work out what our past environments were like.

- **Many sedimentary rocks** have great economic significance. Coal was the power behind the Industrial Revolution, and is still an important fuel, used for generating electricity.

- **Our knowledge** of evolution is based on fossil records. Fossils are preserved in sedimentary rocks.

- **Some well-known sedimentary rocks** include sandstone, limestone, mudstone, or shale.

▼ *These high sea cliffs are made of sedimentary sandstone. The strata run almost horizontally.*

Weathering

▪ **Rocks exposed** on the Earth's surface are broken down in many ways. Weathering causes rock decomposition without involving any movement, or transportation.

▪ **Weathering** is the first of many processes of denudation (wearing away). These processes result in an overall lowering of the land surface.

▪ **Many external agents** are involved in weathering, including temperature changes, rain, wind, bacteria, animals, and plants.

▪ **Weathering** produces the particles of rocks and minerals, which are then transported and deposited as sedimentary rocks.

▪ **Mechanical weathering** is mainly the result of temperature changes. Water in cracks and joints in rocks expands when it freezes. This creates stresses, which cause rock disintegration. At the base of many mountain slopes and cliffs are scree slopes made of mechanically weathered fragments.

▶ When rocks are heated and cooled in deserts, flakes break off to leave a rounded core.

◄ *Tree roots may grow into joints in rocks. As the roots get larger, the rock is broken up.*

Temperature changes can cause the different minerals in a rock to expand and contract at different rates. Stress produced in this way may lead to thin sheets of rock peeling off like the skin of an onion.

Chemical weathering affects many rocks. Limestones are particularly vulnerable. Rainwater is a mild, natural carbonic acid, and with increased acid rain, it becomes more acidic.

Limestone itself is not soluble in rainwater. Calcium carbonate, of which limestones are largely composed, reacts with acid rainwater and soluble calcium bicarbonate is produced.

Granite, often regarded as indestructible, is far from it. The most common mineral in granite is feldspar, which is easily weathered by acid water, especially in tropical conditions. The feldspar rots to clay and the granite is reduced to an incoherent mass of quartz and mica sand.

► *In cold climates, water in cracks in the rock turns to ice, breaking the rock apart.*

55

Erosion

The breakdown of rocks and wearing away of the land surface by processes that involve movement is called erosion.

There are many different environments in which erosion takes place, including rivers, glaciers, seas, and deserts.

River erosion occurs mainly where powerful, rapidly flowing streams cut deep valleys through the landscape. The valley sides are eroded, as is the rock debris carried by the water current. Much eroded sediment is carried to the sea where it is then deposited.

The power of river erosion is well demonstrated by the depth to which the Colorado River has cut its deep V-shaped canyons in Arizona.

A glacier is less fluid than water, and so erodes a deep, reasonably straight valley that has a U-shaped profile. Eroded rock is carried on and within the ice, and deposited when the ice melts.

◄ The Grand Canyon in Arizona is a massive gorge cut by the Colorado River. It is about 280 mi long, and in areas it is up to 18 mi wide and one mile deep.

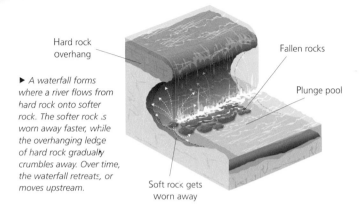

Hard rock overhang

Fallen rocks

Plunge pool

▶ *A waterfall forms where a river flows from hard rock onto softer rock. The softer rock is worn away faster, while the overhanging ledge of hard rock gradually crumbles away. Over time, the waterfall retreats, or moves upstream.*

Soft rock gets worn away

- **As a glacier moves**, rocks frozen into the ice scrape at the bedrock, eroding marks called striations into it. The ice freezes into cracks in the valley sides and plucks rock fragments away as it moves.

- **At the coast**, waves containing sand and pebbles break against cliffs and scour rock pavements. Cliffs are further reduced by landsliding, often assisted by water running over the cliff face or seeping from rocks.

- **In desert regions**, because of the lack of vegetation, the wind is the major erosive factor. Sand picked up by the wind blasts at any upstanding rock masses, concentrating near ground level. Rock pillars are sculpted by this abrasive wind, the weaker strata being eaten away more readily.

- **Larger rock fragments**, which are too heavy to be picked up by the wind, are etched and eroded into three-sided "dreikanter." Such pebbles are well known from ancient sandstone deposits, and indicate a wind-dominant environment in the distant past.

How sedimentary rocks are formed

🔹 **Weathering and erosion** provide the particles from which sedimentary rocks are made.

🔹 **Sediments** may form into rocks with no alteration, by a process called lithification. When physical or chemical changes occur during rock formation, the process is called diagenesis.

🔹 **Most sediment** is deposited in the sea. Initially it will be wet and the pore spaces between the grains fill with water. This must be removed to turn the sediment into rock.

🔹 **As layer after layer** of sediment is deposited, the weight and pressure produced begins to affect lower layers. Water may be squeezed out, and the individual grains get packed together more tightly, reducing pore space.

🔹 **When sediment** is first deposited in water, most of it (70–90 percent) is made up of small gaps between the grains. These gaps are called pore spores. As the sediment is buried deeper in the Earth's crust, the pore spores are reduced to only around 30 percent of the rock's volume.

🔹 **Many rocks**, such as sandstone, do remain porous and may be a valuable source of underground water, gas, or oil.

🔹 **Mineral enriched fluids** seep into pore spaces and form natural cements that bind together the individual particles, including pebbles, in sedimentary rocks. A common cement is calcite (calcium carbonate).

In some cases, where overlying weight is considerable, sand grains may become welded together, with the removal of pore spaces.

Quartz (silicon dioxide) is another common cementing mineral. This hard, chemically resistant cement is common in many sandstones.

Limestones are largely made of calcite, often derived from organic matter. They may be packed with shell fragments, broken crinoid stems, or corals. Recrystallization may occur and the organic material is dissolved, to be replaced by a mosaic of crystalline calcite.

Many sediments undergo color changes as they harden. Iron compounds seeping into pore spaces may color sandstone red or yellow.

▶ These layers of sand and pebbles may one day become sandstone and breccia.

Sandstone

Sandstone is a common sedimentary rock. Essentially, it is made of sand grains compressed together, or cemented by other minerals.

Sandstones can be created in a variety of environments. Some are formed in deserts, some on the seabed, and others in rivers and deltas.

Sand grains blown by the wind tend to be rounded and slightly frosted in appearance. Those carried and deposited by water are usually more angular.

The main mineral in sandstone is quartz. This material is chemically and physically resistant, so is readily able to withstand being transported some distance before being deposited.

The main minerals in andesite are plagioclase feldspar, pyroxene, amphibole, biotite, and mica.

◄ The sandstone in these strata is red-colored because of hematite (iron oxide) on the quartz grains.

- **Some sandstones** contain a relatively high proportion of feldspar. One example is a rock called arkose. Feldspar is easily weathered, so its presence in sandstone suggests that the sediment was deposited quickly.

DID YOU KNOW?
On the bedding planes of certain sandstones small glittery flakes can be seen. These are fragments of the mineral called mica.

- **Sandstones** generally do not contain as many fossils as other sedimentary rocks such as limestones. However, sandstones formed in the sea can contain mollusk and brachiopod shells, trilobites, and ammonites. Delta sandstones contain plant fossils and some of the best dinosaur fossils are from sandstones formed in riverbeds and on land.

- **There are many** color varieties of sandstone. These are mainly due to minerals in the rock, some of which cement the sand grains together.

- **Red and yellow** sandstones contain the minerals hematite and limonite around their grains.

- **Sandstones** are economically important. They are used for building as many of them can be cut easily into stones. Porous sandstones can hold water, oil, or gas underground, which can be extracted by means of boreholes.

▶ *The small, rounded quartz grains making this sandstone are clearly seen in this specimen.*

61

Strata and folding

🔹 **Many sedimentary rocks** are deposited in neat layers that geologists call strata. Each stratum represents the seabed or land surface at the time it was deposited. The term "bedding planes" is also used for strata.

🔹 **Fossils** may be found on strata. When deposition stops for any length of time, animals and plants may live on the sediment surface, and their remains will be covered over and preserved when deposition resumes.

🔹 **One of the main** principles of geology is that as strata are formed, the oldest one, the first to be deposited, will be at the bottom and the youngest, the most recently formed, will be at the top.

▼ *When rocks are highly compressed, tight folds can be formed.*

- **If there is continuous** deposition of sediment, then there will be no strata. Sedimentary rocks without strata are said to be massive.

DID YOU KNOW?
Compression of the crust buckles strata into upfolds (anticlines) and downfolds (synclines).

- **Strata** can be linked from place to place by using the fossils they contain. The same ammonite fossils found in mudstone in Greenland, shale in Argentina, and limestone in Italy prove that these strata are the same age.

- **The layers of** sedimentary rock were originally deposited horizontally. As the Earth's crust moves, so these layers may be tilted and folded.

- **Though many younger** strata are more or less horizontal, older ones are usually folded. However, the Torridonian sandstones in northwest Scotland, UK, are more than 900 million years old and have never been folded.

- **Geologists** measure features of folded strata when they make geological maps. The greatest angle that can be measured down a sloping stratum is called the dip of the stratum. This is indicated on a geological map with a small arrow pointing in the direction of the dip and a figure for the angle.

- **When the pressure** is greater from one direction, the folding will be uneven and one side of the fold may even tilt over above the other. This is a recumbent fold. Structures such as these are common in the great mountain ranges such as the Alps and the Andes.

Conglomerate and breccia

- **Conglomerate** is the name geologists give to a sedimentary rock made of large, rounded fragments.

- **Usually, the pebbles** and other fragments are held together with a cement. This may be quartz, calcite, or iron compounds.

- **The pebbles** themselves can be made of many materials. There may be rock fragments that have been eroded and heaped together. Many conglomerates contain pebbles of quartz or quartzite.

- **Conglomerates** are usually deposited near to the area from which their fragments were eroded. Many conglomerates were deposited by rivers. This is because it takes a powerful river current to move such large particles.

- **Many conglomerates** are beach deposits. The fragments will be well-rounded because of being rolled backward and forward by the waves and tide.

◄ Breccia is made of large, angular rock fragments cemented together.

- **Some conglomerates** are the deposits of flash floods in predominantly arid areas. Great masses of sand and pebbles lying on the land surface are easily washed along by powerful floods.

- **Breccia** is a rock that is similar to a conglomerate. However in breccia, the fragments are jagged and angular.

- **Breccia** is deposited very quickly, sometimes without water transport, so the pebbles and other fragments it contains don't get worn and rounded.

- **Many breccias** are formed as scree by the weathering of high mountain slopes.

- **Rock fragments** are produced when rocks move relatively to each other during faulting. The jumble of broken rock along the fault line is called fault breccia.

▲ These layers of conglomerate were formed on a river floodplain, when masses of pebbles were carried and deposited by turbulent water, more than 200 mya.

Limestone

◀ *Limestone is often packed with fossils. Those shown here are the remains of water snails.*

Limestone is a sedimentary rock that contains a high proportion of the mineral calcite (calcium carbonate). Often, this is of organic origin.

Limestones are usually pale-colored, being gray, cream, brownish, or buff. Some are very dark and may be almost black because of a high percentage of mud and other eroded sediment.

Fossils are abundant in most limestones. Some of these rocks are named after the fossils they contain. Coral limestone, crinoidal, and shelly limestone are rich in these fossils. Limestone may be a mass of fossils cemented together by calcite.

Most limestone deposits are geologically young. Organisms that developed hard calcite shells, from which the rock is often made, didn't evolve until Cambrian times. Pre-Cambrian limestone is often made of calcite secreted by colonies of blue-green algae, forming mounds called stromatolites.

Chemical weathering easily attacks limestone. The rock is etched into characteristic structures, and joints are enlarged as water runs through them. Underground cave and stream systems develop.

Dolostone (dolomite) is a type of limestone in which much of the calcite has been changed into the mineral dolomite. Dolomite is a double carbonate of calcium and magnesium.

Oolitic limestone is made of small, rounded grains (ooliths) of sediment, about 2–3 mm in diameter. Made of concentric layers of calcite, these are of chemical origin. The layers are formed around a shell fragment or sand grain. Today, oolitic limestones are forming around the Bahama Banks in the Caribbean.

Reef limestones are fossilized sediment reefs. They contain a variety of fossils of organisms that live in the shallow reef environment. These may include corals, trilobites, brachiopods, mollusks, and crinoids.

The reef itself is a mound of sediment, the surface of which is near to sea level. Some reefs may be composed of a lime mud, secreted by various microorganisms.

Limestone has many important economic uses and is often extensively quarried. For many years it has been powdered for agricultural purposes. Limestone is an important building stone and forms the basis of cement.

▼ *Limestone landscapes often have much bare rock. This is because there is very little surface water so soil doesn't form and plants cannot grow.*

Limestone pavement

🔖 **A limestone pavement** is an expanse of bare limestone that has taken thousands of years to develop and is usually crisscrossed by deep grooves.

🔖 **In the British Isles**, limestone pavements are best known in the Yorkshire Dales and the Burren region of western Ireland.

🔖 **Limestone pavements form** a significant landscape feature, and the deep cracks or fissures running through them, called grikes, are places where rare limestone-loving plants grow. The blocks of limestone between the grikes are called clints.

▼ *In this limestone pavement in the Pennines of North Yorkshire, UK, the blocks of limestone called clints **1** are separated from each other by deep cracks called grikes **2**.*

1   2

- **In recent years**, many limestone pavements have been destroyed. The limestone has been removed and sold for rockery and building stone.

- **The landscape features** of regions where limestone occurs at the surface owe their formation to the physical and chemical properties of the rock.

- **Limestone is mainly composed** of the mineral calcite, with the chemical composition of calcium carbonate.

- **Chemical weathering** of limestone is concentrated along bedding planes and vertical joints. These are enlarged, and surface water easily runs underground. Such rocks are said to be permeable.

- **Surface water is lacking** in many limestone regions, which means soil development and plant growth are very limited, and bare rock occurs at the surface.

- **It has been argued** that some limestone pavements formed below a surface layer of soil and peat. This would increase the acidity of water running through the limestone. At a later time, possibly after the last ice age, the peat was weathered and eroded to leave the bare limestone surface.

DID YOU KNOW?

Calcite reacts chemically with weak acids in rainwater and ground water to form calcium bicarbonate. This chemical compound is soluble in water, and so limestone is chemically weathered and removed.

Chalk

🔹 **A special type of limestone**, chalk is almost pure white. It is very fine-grained and most contains more than 90 percent calcium carbonate (calcite).

🔹 **Chalk** is a sedimentary rock that was deposited in the sea, probably away from the continental shelf, in regions where there was little seabed disturbance.

🔹 **Most chalk** occurs in western Europe and in some parts of North America, for example in the state of Kansas. European chalk was deposited during the Cretaceous Period between 142 and 65 mya.

🔹 **The famous white cliffs** along the south coast of England, UK, which for years have been a landmark for travelers, are composed of chalk.

🔹 **One of the puzzles** about chalk is its great purity. There is an almost complete lack of sand or mud and other sediment carried from the land.

🔹 **Much of the nearest land** was probably very low-lying, without hills and mountains. Because of this there would have been very little erosion bringing mud or sand into the sea.

◀ *Chalk is a white powdery rock made of the remains of minute sea creatures.*

▲ *Some types of chalk rocks are almost entirely made of the fossils of small sea creatures.*

🔹 **Virtually all the calcite** in chalk is the remains of small organisms. These include microscopic creatures called coccoliths.

🔹 **Large fossils** are found in chalk. These include ammonites and other mollusks, brachiopods, and echinoids (sea urchins).

🔹 **The layers of chalk** are divided into time zones using ammonite fossils.

🔹 **A variety of creatures** lived in and on the soft seabed. Worms and sea urchins burrowed into the chalky mud. Sponges and mollusks also lived on the seabed.

Flint

◀ When carefully chipped, flint can be used to make tools such as this pointed hand ax.

🔹 **A hard, nodular rock**, flint is found in irregular layers in chalk.

🔹 **Flints** can be seen in chalk cliffs as dark parallel bands running among the white strata.

🔹 **Like the common mineral quartz**, flint is composed of silicon dioxide. Quartz usually forms hexagonal crystals but flint is different. The crystals making up flint are so small that a powerful microscope is needed to see them.

🔹 **The silica** in flint is derived from small sea creatures. It mainly comes from the internal supports of sponges. It is believed that concentrations of silica formed within the chalk sediment and hardened into flint.

🔹 **Large fossils** are sometimes replaced by flint, such as the heart-shaped sea urchin called *Micraster*.

🔹 **"False flints"** are hollow inside. The silica formed around a sponge, that eventually disintegrated, leaving a hollow. These false flints have a white powdery interior made from the shells of single-celled foraminferans and ostracods (creatures related to water fleas).

When flint is seen on the surface of a chalk stratum, the nodular lumps may occur in rings.

Flint is so hard that it can't be scratched with a knife blade. It breaks easily into curved shapes with very sharp edges.

The durability and sharpness of broken flint has been exploited in the past.

Early man used flints to make hand axes from at least 2 mya. These were shaped by chipping flakes of flint from around a core, using a hammer stone. Flint has continued to be used in tools right up until the early 1800s when flintlocks were still being made.

▶ Flint is often dark colored and breaks with sharp jagged edges. It is a very pure type of silicon dioxide.

Ice age rocks

◀ **The most recent ice age** ended in Britain and most of Europe and North America around 10,000 years ago. Much evidence for this ice age can be found in the landforms created by the ice sheets and glaciers and in their special sedimentary rocks.

◀ **Glacial rocks** are known from much older times. Glacial sediments occur in Brazil that were formed during the Carboniferous and Permian Periods (355–250 mya). These are 5,250 ft thick in places, suggesting an amazing amount of erosion by the ancient glaciers.

◀ **A typical feature** of many glacial sedimentary rocks is that they are badly sorted. This means that within one deposit there will be fragments of many sizes, from fine clay to large boulders.

◀ **Glacial rocks** are commonly unbedded. They do not have the neat strata that identify most sedimentary rocks.

◀ **The term moraine** is used to cover a variety of glacial deposits. It may consist of sand, gravel, clay, and rock fragments. Eroded rock debris falls along the sides of a glacier. This lateral moraine may be further eroded against the valley sides as the ice moves.

◀ **A push moraine** is bulldozed along at the glacier snout (front end). Any glacier may produce a number of these as it retreats and then returns. Terminal moraines usually form in this way, and give geologists evidence about the furthest position a glacier reached.

- **If two valley glaciers** join, their lateral moraines will merge to form a medial moraine in the new, larger glacier.

- **Much meltwater** is associated with glaciers. This flows out from under the ice and carries sediment. Usually meltwater is thick and milky-looking because of the clay it contains. The area in front of the glacier snout is called an outwash plain. Water-formed sediments occur here, often in neat strata.

- **The large boulders** (and other rocks) carried and dumped by the ice are often left stranded and out of place. These are called erratics, and their significance is considerable. By studying the erratics, geologists are able to tell from where a long-vanished ice sheet came.

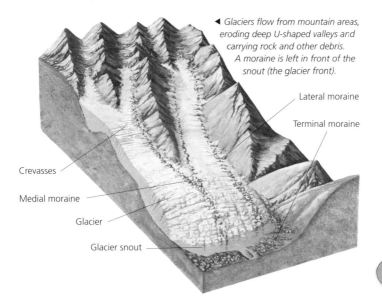

◀ Glaciers flow from mountain areas, eroding deep U-shaped valleys and carrying rock and other debris. A moraine is left in front of the snout (the glacier front).

Lateral moraine

Terminal moraine

Crevasses

Medial moraine

Glacier

Glacier snout

Coal

- **A fossil fuel**, coal provided power to the 19th century Industrial Revolution. It is the most abundant and easiest fossil fuel to recover.

- **Coal is the consolidated remains** of carbon stored in plants. These plants, living hundreds of millions of years ago, took in energy from sunlight and stored it in their tissues. When a light bulb is switched on, using electricity generated in a coal-fired power station, "fossil sunlight" is being released.

- **Coal** is most common in strata of the Carboniferous Period (355–298 mya). It is found in rocks from the Permian Period (298–250 mya) in South Africa, Brazil, China, and Australia, and in rocks from the Triassic Period (250–208 mya) in China and eastern U.S.

- **Coal from** the Jurassic Period (208–144 mya) has been mined in England, UK, northeast Scotland, UK, Siberia, and China. Rocks containing coal from the Cretaceous Period (144–65 mya) occur in Siberia, northern Germany, and Canada.

- **The coal-forming plants** of the Carboniferous Period developed from peat deposited in the sedimentary layers of sand and mud formed on a vast delta.

- **Peat** is the first stage in the development of coal. This is a brown, often very waterlogged, material that has formed from partially decayed plant matter. For peat to be a useful fuel, it has to be cut into blocks and dried.

DID YOU KNOW?
At the present rate of use, coal will long outlast oil and gas as a fossil fuel resource.

In some parts of the world, peat is used for domestic heating. It is burned in power stations in some countries, such as Ireland.

As peat is buried under more accumulated sediment, it becomes compressed and heated. The increase in temperature drives off impurities, including water. Gradually, the percentage of carbon in the peat increases, and it becomes (brown) lignite and then coal.

Bituminous coal contains a far higher percentage of carbon than lignite and is the most widely used coal, but produces much ash.

▼ Most coal was created from trees and other vegetation living in swampy conditions. The dead trees formed peat as they rotted very slowly and eventually after being buried and heated under thousands of feet of rock, the peat turned to coal.

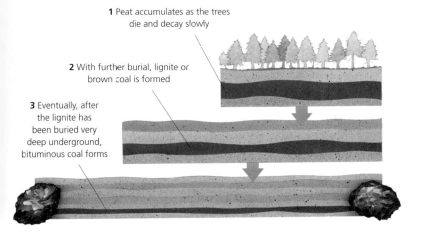

1 Peat accumulates as the trees die and decay slowly

2 With further burial, lignite or brown coal is formed

3 Eventually, after the lignite has been buried very deep underground, bituminous coal forms

Oil and gas

🔹 **Oil and gas** are fossil fuels. Natural gas, commonly found with oil, has in many places taken over from coal gas as an important domestic and industrial fuel.

🔹 **Oil** has given wealth to many nations that otherwise were poor.

🔹 **Oil is a mixture** of many different hydrocarbons (compounds made largely of hydrogen and carbon) from marine organisms.

🔹 **Oil and gas** are very mobile and move, under pressure, through strata, away from where they were formed.

🔹 **Usually**, **oil and gas** are "trapped" below ground. They move upward through porous or permeable strata. Limestone and sandstone are good at allowing this movement. Eventually the moving fluids may come to a nonporous layer such as mudstone. Their movement is halted. The oil and gas then accumulate in the porous strata below the cap rock in an oil "trap."

🔹 **The strata** containing oil often lie on top of strata containing brine (highly salted water) and gas occurs above the oil-rich layer.

◀ *Significant reserves of oil and gas have been discovered in the rock under the seabed. The fossil fuel is obtained using oil rigs—large platforms anchored to the seabed.*

◀ A "nodding donkey" pumps oil from Jurassic strata.

🔺 **Oil and gas** may eventually leak out onto the Earth's surface. When this happens, no geological exploration and surveying is needed to find the fossil fuels.

🔺 **Oil does not always flow** up to the surface, and in many oilfields it has to be pumped to the surface by machines called "nodding donkeys."

🔺 **When geologists** go out prospecting for oil, they look for structures where oil may be trapped. Areas where there is little soil and vegetation can be photographed from the air and structures show up readily. On the ground, porous strata can be detected below the surface by measuring the electrical resistance of rocks or their reaction to shock waves from small explosions.

🔺 **Most oil** is discovered by drilling boreholes. Drilling for oil requires a lubricant called drilling mud. This keeps the drill bit cool. It is commonly made of heavy minerals and volcanic clay.

🔺 **In some areas** such as the North Sea, oil was not found in the areas first prospected. Gas was present, however, and this became an important resource in the 1960s.

Evaporite rocks

◀ **The term "evaporite"** is used for a range of rocks deposited from salt water. Rock salt (halite), rock gypsum, and potash are the three most common and economically important evaporite rocks. Geologists classify all these deposits as chemical rocks.

◀ **The main evaporite deposits** exploited for their chemicals are formed from minerals in sea water.

◀ **If part of the sea**, such as a bay or gulf, is cut off from the open ocean by a sand bank, it will begin to dry up, especially in a hot, dry climate. This is the start of evaporite formation.

◀ **Some evaporite deposits** occur where inland salt lakes have dried out.

◀ **In the sea**, a series of evaporite rocks is deposited in a definite sequence. The rocks are usually interbedded with mudstone, which contains a high amount of calcite (calcium carbonate).

◀ **Many evaporite deposits** are forming at the present time, especially in arid regions. These are usually processed where they occur.

▼ Potash is mined and used on a large scale for making agricultural fertilizers.

▲ *Enclosed basins of salt water are used to produce halite, or rock salt. As the water in each basin evaporates, crystals of salt are formed.*

 Some of the evaporite chemicals are more soluble in water than others. The least soluble form layers of rock first. The most soluble remain in solution until the water has virtually dried out. The first to occur as strata are often gypsum and anhydrite. Rock salt is the next to form, and finally a mixture of potash rocks.

Of the marine evaporates, rock salt (halite) is essential for human and animal health. It has been in great demand for thousands of years as a food enhancer and preserver. Gypsum and anhydrite are used for making sulfuric acid and fertilizers and for plaster and plasterboard. Potash is used as the basis of agricultural fertilizers.

The evaporites deposited in land-bound lakes include borax and nitrates. Borax is used in glass, paper, and leather products. Nitrates are the basis of fertilizers, explosives, and nitric acid.

In Britain there are considerable evaporite (halite) deposits in Cheshire and also in North Yorkshire, where mines more than 3 mi deep go out under the North Sea. Other important deposits occur in Germany, the U.S., and Chile.

Stalactites and stalagmites

The roofs of many limestone caves are covered with hanging, icicle-shaped growths made of calcium carbonate. These are called stalactites. The structures growing on the cave floor are stalagmites.

Limestone, which is a common sedimentary rock, is easily weathered by chemical processes. Acid rainwater changes the calcite in limestone into soluble calcium bicarbonate, which is carried away.

▼ *Stalactites are formed when lime-rich water that drips from a cave roof deposits minerals. This creates the hanging icicle-like structures. Underneath the stalactites, stumpy stalagmites develop.*

- **Chemical weathering** of limestone along bedding planes and joints allows water to run underground. Passages are eroded by this water, and as they grow in size, cave systems develop.

DID YOU KNOW?
In western Ireland, a stalactite has been found that is 21 ft long.

- **In the British Isles**, limestone caves have been formed in northwest Scotland, Derbyshire, North Yorkshire, Gloucestershire, Devon, and western Ireland.

- **The opening** on the surface down which water runs is called a pothole. Gaping Gill pothole in North Yorkshire, UK, is 395 ft deep.

- **Water dripping** from a limestone cave roof is full of dissolved calcium bicarbonate. This is deposited as calcium carbonate (calcite) as the water drips into the cave and in part evaporates. The calcite is deposited in concentric rings to form stalactites.

- **Stalagmites** usually form beneath a stalactite from water dripping off its tip. They are more stumpy and shorter.

- **Stalactites** hanging from the cave roof tend to be slender. Some, known as straw stalactites, are very small, but some are huge and can grow to many feet in length.

- **Both structures** are made of many layers of calcite. If cut open, the concentric rings of calcite can be seen. Sometimes, a stalactite and a stalagmite will join together to form a column.

Superposition

- **Geology**, like any science, has a number of laws, or principles, which help scientists to interpret rocks. The principle of superposition is one of these.

- **William Smith** (1769–1839), an English canal engineer and pioneering geologist, established the principle of superposition.

- **In simple terms**, the law of superposition states that in a sequence of sedimentary rocks, the older rocks lie below the younger layers.

- **A geologist** in the field may have problems interpreting strata according to this principle. In extreme conditions, folding for example will overturn the beds of rock so that younger layers lie beneath older ones.

- **Similarly a "thrust fault"** may force old rocks above younger ones, which is another reason why the principle cannot be applied.

- **There are a number** of ways in which a geologist can prove if rocks are the correct "way up." These need to be applied before the order of strata can be determined.

- **Each stratum** marks a break in the deposition of sediment. On its surface various marks may be made. These prove which way up it formed. The sediment may be rippled, like a modern beach. If sediment dried out, mud cracks would be formed.

- **Fossils of animals**, such as mollusk shells in their burrows, can also be used to show whether the rocks are the correct way up.

- **Volcanic rocks** that contained much gas will have their vesicles (gas-bubble holes) at the top of a lava flow.

▼ On this wave-cut platform, the older strata are closer to the sea and youngest ones toward the land. Each stratum dips (slopes) landward and disappears below a younger (higher) layer

85

Ironstones

🔸 **At least 90 percent** of all the iron mined and quarried each year is in the form of the sedimentary rock called ironstone.

🔸 **Ironstones** formed in shallow water in the sea, near to land.

🔸 **Iron** is one of the most sought after metals. It is used in the manufacture of steel, the main uses of which are in building and vehicle production.

▼ *Banded ironstone is one of the richest ores of iron. This example comes from Western Australia.*

- **The presence of iron** compounds in sedimentary rocks colors them red or yellowish-brown.

- **Some types of iron** are soluble in water and are carried to areas where sedimentary rocks are being deposited.

- **Iron** is easily oxidized (rusted) so is not very stable in today's climate. In the Precambrian Era (more than 600 mya), there was very little oxygen in the atmosphere, as there were no true land plants. Iron compounds were more stable at this time.

  - **Precambrian ironstones** are called banded ironstones because of their structure. They have thin, alternating layers of chert (a form of silicon dioxide) and iron oxide. These ores may contain up to 65 percent iron.

  - **The ironstones** on which heavy industry was founded during the 19th century are of relatively low iron content—often less than 30 percent iron.

- **Many ironstones** have an oolitic structure, being made of small, rounded grains coated with iron minerals.

Desert rocks

- **Deserts** are arid regions that receive very low rainfall, usually not enough to support vegetation.

- **Most desert regions** are areas of high temperatures, but Antarctica is also a desert.

- **By studying** the sediments and other features of today's deserts, geologists can work out which rocks were formed in ancient deserts.

- **Sandstone** is one of the main desert rocks. The grains are rounded by wind action.

- **The strata** formed by the wind are not horizontal. Instead, curved "cross-bedded" layers are formed.

- **Larger fragments** of quartz are often pitted and frosted by sand blasting.

- **Deserts are very windy** environments, so mica, a mineral that occurs in small flakes, is absent from desert rocks.

- **If rain does fall** on a desert region, it is usually very heavy for a short time. This creates flash floods, which can carry sand, pebbles, and boulders.

- **Desert rose** is a flowerlike formation of the mineral gypsum that forms in deserts.

◄ Monument Valley in Utah is made up of sandstone buttes, the eroded stumps of mountains.

Metamorphic rocks

- **Metamorphic rocks** are any rocks that have been changed by heat, pressure, or a combination of these forces.

- **Most metamorphic changes** occur at temperatures of between 392°F and 1,292°F. The extreme pressure at which rocks metamorphose is up to 6,000 times greater than atmospheric pressure and can occur at a depth of 12 mi.

- **Contact metamorphism** involves only heat. Regional metamorphism is brought about by heat and pressure.

- **No melting of rock** occurs during metamorphism. When melting takes place, magma, from which igneous rocks are formed, is created.

- **The chemical composition** and structure of a rock can be changed by metamorphism.

- **When large-scale faulting** occurs, dislocation metamorphism takes place.

- **Original structures,** such as strata in sedimentary rocks, are removed during metamorphism.

◄ Garnet is a mineral that forms in many metamorphic rocks, especially schist. It is used as a gemstone and may be cut and facetted.

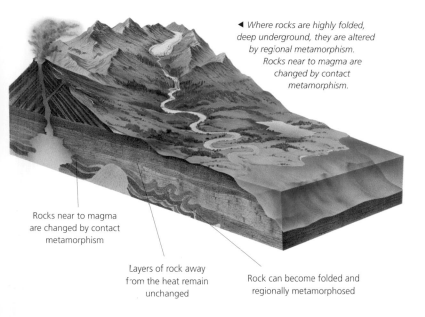

◀ Where rocks are highly folded, deep underground, they are altered by regional metamorphism. Rocks near to magma are changed by contact metamorphism.

Rocks near to magma are changed by contact metamorphism

Layers of rock away from the heat remain unchanged

Rock can become folded and regionally metamorphosed

🔹 **Fossils are sometimes found** in slightly metamorphosed rocks such as slate. As the degree of metamorphism increases, fossils are destroyed.

🔹 **Garnet**, a mineral much used as a gemstone, is common in the metamorphic rock called schist.

🔹 **Some of the oldest rocks** in the Earth's crust are highly metamorphosed gneisses.

Contact metamorphism

🔹 **Contact metamorphism** occurs when rocks are heated by magma or lava.

🔹 **A metamorphic aureole** is the region around a mass of magma in which rocks have been altered.

🔹 **A lava flow** can only metamorphose the rocks lying below it.

🔹 **The amount** of contact metamorphism depends on the size of the igneous body producing heat and any fluids seeping from it.

🔹 **The metamorphic aureole** around a large batholith may be a few miles wide.

🔹 **A small sill**, dike, or lava flow may metamorphose rocks up to only a few inches away.

🔹 **A gradual** metamorphic change takes place away from the igneous intrusion. The rocks furthest away are only slightly metamorphosed. Right next to the intrusion they may be highly altered.

🔹 **Dark-colored "spots"** and clusters of minerals are a common feature of clay and shale that have been altered by contact metamorphism. With great heat, a tough rock called hornfels is formed.

🔹 **When heated**, limestone becomes crystalline marble. This new rock is a mosaic of calcite crystals, often with veins of green or blue minerals.

🔹 **Sandstone** is changed to a hard, crystalline rock called metaquartzite.

▼ *The sloping rock surface (shown right) is made of granite. When it formed deep underground nearly 300 mya, intense heat from the magma metamorphosed the dark hornfels (shown left). The contact between the two different rocks is clearly seen.*

Marble

▼ *The most iconic part of the Taj Mahal building is the large, marble dome, which measures 115 ft in height.*

- **Marble is formed** by the contact metamorphism of limestone.

- **Heat** from an igneous intrusion or lava flow causes the calcite in the limestone to recrystallize.

- **Original features** in the limestone, such as strata and fossils, are destroyed, and an interlocking mosaic of calcite crystals forms.

- **Pure limestones** become very pale, often sugary, marbles, with very little color veining.

- **Limestone** that has impurities in the form of clay, other sedimentary material, and minerals are changed into colorfully veined marbles.

- **The metamorphic minerals** brucite, olivine, and serpentine can give marble a greenish coloring.

- **For more than 2,500 years**, marble has been prized as a decorative stone. This is because it is easily shaped and polished, and has attractive coloring.

- **In the classical Greek** and Roman periods, marble was the main rock used for statues.

- **Michelangelo's** *David*, carved between 1501 and 1504, is one of the most well-known marble statues in existence.

DID YOU KNOW?
Olivine marble has small patches of bright green or brown olivine. This is a silicate mineral formed by the heat of metamorphism.

Metaquartzite

🔹 **When sandstone** is altered by contact metamorphism, it turns into metaquartzite.

🔹 **Heat from** an igneous intrusion or lava flow causes the quartz grains in sandstone to grow and fuse together or recrystallize.

🔹 **Metaquartzite** may have only faint traces of the original bedding, and any fossils in the original sandstone will have been destroyed.

🔹 **Sandstone** is more resistant to metamorphic change than many other rocks because so much heat is needed to alter it.

🔹 **Metaquartzite** is a pale-colored rock, often with a sugary texture.

🔹 **Sandstone** is a porous rock with small spaces between the grains. Metaquartzite is crystalline and nonporous.

🔹 **Because it is largely made** of quartz, metaquartzite is a very hard rock. It is resistant to weathering.

🔹 **Metaquartzite is quarried** and used in the construction industry.

◀ *Originally sandstone, this metaquartzite is now a mosaic of quartz crystals. The original layers in the rock have disappeared.*

▲ The pale-colored metaquartzite in this cliff still has some of its original features—strata are visible.

🔹 **Metaquartzite is found** very close to large batholiths. Smaller intrusions rarely have sufficient heat to change quartz-rich sandstone.

🔹 **Though it is virtually 100 percent quartz,** metaquartzite may contain feldspar and iron oxides in small amounts.

Hornfels

- **Formed by the action of direct heat** on pre-existing rocks, hornfels is a metamorphic rock.

- **This rock often occurs** very close to igneous rocks such as granite. The granitic magma is a source of great heat when it is being intruded.

▼ This hornfels in Cornwall, UK, has been twisted and folded on a small scale by pressure in the Earth's crust. The paler bands are rich in quartz.

- **As well as heat**, high temperature liquids can seep from granitic magma and help to metamorphose the surrounding rocks.

- **Hornfels is a flinty, tough rock** that breaks unevenly, often with jagged edges.

- **The exact composition of hornfels** depends to a certain extent on the original premetamorphic rock. Usually quartz is a common mineral, along with mica.

- **This rock has medium** to fine crystals, often with a granular texture.

- **Hornfels can be twisted** and contorted into tight folds.

- **The conditions of metamorphism** cause new minerals to form. These include cordierite, chiastolite, and garnet.

- **Some minerals, including garnet and pyroxene**, often occur in what geologists call porphyroblasts. These are isolated clusters of minerals within the hornfels.

Faulting

DID YOU KNOW?
A thrust fault can move huge masses of rock many tens of miles up a very low angled fault plane.

◀ **Faults** are breaks in the rocks of the Earth's crust where the rocks move relative to each other. The same stratum will be at a different level on each side of the fault.

◀ **A joint** is a break in the rocks where no movement takes place.

◀ **Both faults and joints** are often the places where hot, mineral-rich fluids rise through the crust. Important mineral reserves occur in this way.

◀ **The actual surface** where the rocks break and move is called the fault plane. In many faults, such as normal and reverse faults, the fault plane is very steep. Thrust faults have a fault plane sloping at only a few degrees.

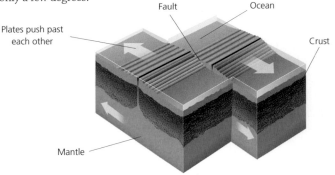

Fault　　Ocean

Plates push past each other

Crust

Mantle

▲ When two plates push past each other, pressure can build up, creating a break, or fault, which often causes an earthquake. Some earthquakes are so powerful that buildings collapse.

- **When faults move**, earthquakes occur. Movement on the San Andreas Fault that runs through California threatens large cities such as Los Angeles.

- **A normal fault** is where the Earth's crust stretches and one mass of rock moves down a break—the fault plane.

- **If two normal faults** occur parallel to each other, a block of the crust may sink between them. This is called a rift, or graben. The region of rift valleys in east Africa was formed in this way.

- **Where a reverse fault** occurs, the Earth's crust is made thicker by compression. One mass of rock is forced up the fault plane relative to the rocks on the other side.

- **In a tear fault**, there is virtually no vertical movement. Rock masses are moved sideways relative to each other.

▼ *The San Andreas Fault in California is visible on the Earth's surface.*

Regional metamorphism

- **As the name implies**, this type of metamorphism occurs over great areas of the Earth's crust.

- **Regional metamorphism** happens when mountain building, often associated with movement of the Earth's lithospheric plates, occurs.

- **Pressure and heat** are involved in altering rocks by regional metamorphism.

- **The changes** that take place during regional metamorphism may take tens of millions of years to occur.

- **Some of the oldest rocks** in the Earth's crust have been affected by regional metamorphism. These have been radiometrically dated at more than 3,500 million years old.

- **The deeper** into the crust that rocks are taken by the processes of mountain building, the higher the degree, or grade, of metamorphism they suffer.

- **Rocks** formed by regional metamorphism are identified by their texture. Because of stresses in the rock, minerals are streaked out in layers.

- **High-grade rocks**—those that are altered most—are called gneiss. With increased temperature, caused by depth of burial, melting may occur and magma is created.

- **At lower depths**, where the temperature and pressure are lower, a rock called schist is formed.

▲ Regional metamorphism occurs in the roots of mountain chains. Deep below the Alps in Switzerland, slate, schist, and gneiss are forming.

Around the margins of the mountain region, temperatures are very low. Here, pressure is also low and rocks such as slate are created.

Slate

- **Slate forms** around the margins of mountain regions where the lowest grade of regional metamorphism occurs.

- **Slates** are dark-colored rocks made of grains and crystals too small to be seen with the naked eye.

- **The most recognizable feature** of slate is its cleavage. This is the way the rock splits into thin, neat layers. However, the most weakly metamorphosed slates may not have developed a cleavage

- **Because it splits** so easily, slate has been used for hundreds of years for roofing and gravestones.

- **Fossils** may still be present in slate. These are often squashed or stretched by the stresses that metamorphosed the rock.

Shale

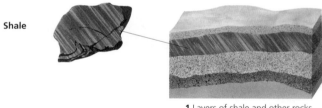

1 Layers of shale and other rocks

Slate

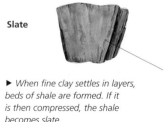

▶ When fine clay settles in layers, beds of shale are formed. If it is then compressed, the shale becomes slate.

2 Pressure caused by folding changes shale to slate

- **Slate** forms from the weak metamorphism of mudstone or siltstone.

- **Small, golden-colored crystals** of pyrite (fool's gold) form in some slates.

- **Green slate** is colored by the mineral chlorite, which grows under metamorphic stress.

- **Some of the world's** most important slate quarries are in North Wales, UK. Slate from here has been shipped all over the world.

- **Slate** is also found in other parts of Britain, including Cumbria, Scotland, and Devon. Elsewhere in the world, it occurs in California, Onijarvi, Finland, and Vosges, France.

▶ This specimen of slate contains crystals of pyrite (iron sulfide). Pyrite often forms during regional metamorphism. The rock has broken along a cleavage surface.

Schist

- **Schist** forms at higher temperatures and pressures than slate. These conditions occur deeper in the Earth's crust and nearer the center of a mountain region.

- **Schist** is a silvery rock because it contains mica—this may be pale muscovite or dark biotite mica.

- **A typical feature** of schist is a wavy banding (called schistosity) running through the rock. This results from the way minerals have lined up during metamorphism.

- **As well as mica**, this rock contains quartz and feldspar.

- **Many new minerals** can form in schist during metamorphism. These include garnet, kyanite, hornblende, and epidote.

▲ *Schist has wavy bands running through it and this example has reddish garnet crystals.*

- **Because temperatures** and pressure are moderately high when schists form, most rocks are altered.

- **Garnet schists** are a source of the semi-precious gemstone, garnet.

Much schist occurs in the European Alps. Here, the rocks were folded and metamorphosed in mid-Cenozoic times, around 40 mya.

In Britain, schist occurs mainly in the Scottish Highlands, where it was formed during the Caledonian Period of mountain building, around 400 mya.

▼ *The hills and mountains of the Scottish Highlands are largely made of schist.*

107

Gneiss

- **The rock gneiss** is formed by extreme heat and pressure deep within the Earth's crust. Under these conditions any previously formed rock will be completely changed. This is the highest grade of regional metamorphism.

- **During orogenies,** some rocks are buried to the depths at which gneiss forms.

- **Gneiss is characterized** by alternating dark- and light-colored bands of different minerals. The mineral crystals are large enough to detect with the naked eye.

▼ *Gneiss forms a rugged landscape of low gray hills with much bare rock.*

▶ *The typical dark and light bands can be seen in this tightly folded gneiss specimen.*

🔹 **The pale bands** contain lower-density minerals such as quartz and feldspar, while the darker streaks contain denser minerals such as biotite, mica, and hornblende.

🔹 **Some gneisses** may have isolated patches of other minerals such as red garnet. These can look like "eyes" in the rock. This rock is called augen gneiss, from the German *Augen*, meaning eyes.

🔹 **The composition of gneiss** is not very different from that of the igneous rock granite.

🔹 **Gneiss** is generally the oldest rock in the area in which it occurs, and some gneisses have been radiometrically dated to more than 3,000 million years.

🔹 **The major continental** shield areas, such as the Canadian and Eurasian shields, are predominantly made of gneiss, with younger rocks on top.

🔹 **Gneiss** is a very durable rock. Its hardness is exploited in road making, and millions of tons of quarried gneiss boulders are used for coastal defenses.

Eclogite

🔹 **Eclogite** is a rock that forms under high temperature and very high pressure in the deep roots of mountain chains.

🔹 **It is a rare rock** and is important because of what geologists can learn from it about the Earth's composition.

▲ *Eclogite can be a most attractive rock, with masses of red garnet and green pyroxene. This example is from Norway.*

- **Eclogite** contains large crystals easily seen with the naked eye.

- **Eclogite is a dark-colored** rock made of yellowish or green pyroxene and red garnet.

- **Other minerals** that occur in small amounts in eclogite include rutile, pyrite, corundum, and kyanite.

DID YOU KNOW?

The minerals in eclogite may be arranged in alternating bands of different types or randomly scattered throughout its structure.

- **Some eclogites** are found in diamond pipes. They have been taken there from great depth by volcanic activity.

- **Geologists** believe that eclogite gives important information about the rocks at the very base of the Earth's crust, and in the uppermost region of the Earth's mantle.

- **Experiments** have shown that eclogite forms when basalt lava is melted and recrystallized under great pressure.

- **Eclogite** occurs worldwide, especially in California, the European Alps, Japan, and South Africa.

Building stones

- **In most parts of the world**, local stone is used for building. It is often possible to work out what the local geology is like by looking at what buildings, especially older ones, are made from.

- **Some rock types** are especially sought after because they are attractive, hard, or easily cut into usable shapes.

- **Sandstone, limestone**, and ironstone are three sedimentary rocks that are often used for building. Most of these can be cut easily and split along bedding planes. Rock without bedding (massive rock) can be more easily cut into the blocks.

- **Though granite** is more difficult to cut than some sedimentary rocks, it has been quarried for building stone for hundreds of years. It is attractive and has good internal strength for structural supports.

- **Because stone used for buildings** is often cut and transported in large blocks, quarries developed in the 18th and 19th centuries were usually near good transport facilities.

- **The famous Aberdeen** granite quarries and the granite quarries in the Channel Isles and Cornwall were often sited near to the sea to make it easy to transport the quarried rock.

- **Warm-colored limestones** of Jurassic age are used in southern England, UK, for many buildings. The well-known Portland limestone was brought to London from coastal quarries.

- **Limestone is readily attacked** by chemical weathering, and many buildings need restoration work when the stone suffers.

- **Slate is a tough**, easily split rock used for roofing.

- **Polished stone** often decorates the facades of offices and banks. Usually, granite or another coarse-grained igneous rock is used for this purpose.

▼ *The body of this cottage is made of small irregular-shaped nodules of flint, found in nearby chalk strata. The framework, window surrounds, and lintels are brick.*

Minerals

What are minerals?

- **A mineral** is a chemical compound or element that forms naturally in many different ways.

- **Most minerals** form organically, which means that living things play no part in their creation. However, some organic materials, such as amber, are usually classed with minerals.

- **Rocks** are made from minerals. Limestone is made mainly of the mineral calcite (calcium carbonate), and granite contains quartz, mica, and feldspar.

- **Some minerals,** such as gold and diamond, are very valuable as currency or gemstones.

- **Geologists** tell one type of mineral from another by using special tests. Many of these are easy to carry out.

- **Many minerals form** as perfect crystals. There is a great variety of crystal shapes, from simple cubes to complex dodecahedra with twelve faces.

◄ Minerals can be bright colors and have fine crystal shapes. The yellowish mineral is ettringite that forms as six-sided crystals.

- **Minerals** can form irregular or rounded shapes without obvious crystals.

- **Some minerals** are magnetic, others react with acids, and some are too hard to be scratched with a knife blade.

- **As well as occurring** in rocks, minerals form in long narrow bands, called mineral veins, that run through the Earth's crust.

- **Minerals** such as hematite (iron oxide), galena (lead sulfide), and salt (sodium chloride) are important industrial raw materials.

▶ Minerals often occur in veins. Here, a 3-ft-wide quartz vein runs across dark-colored slate.

117

How hard are minerals?

- **Geologists** use a number of tests to tell one mineral from another. The hardness test is very useful in mineral identification.

- **The hardness** of a mineral depends on the strength of the forces that bind the atoms in the mineral together.

- **Gemstones** such as diamond, ruby, sapphire, and emerald are very hard. It is very difficult to scratch or damage them.

- **Mineral hardness** is measured according to how easily a mineral can be scratched. A mineral is tested by scratching it in turn with objects of increasing hardness, including the minerals on the hardness scale.

- **Geologists** use a special scale for measuring mineral hardness. It is called Mohs scale and was devised in 1812 by the German mineralogist Friedrich Mohs. There are ten points on the Mohs scale, each one defined by a well-known mineral.

| 1 | 2 | 3 | 4 | 5 |
| Talc | Gypsum | Calcite | Fluorite | Apatite |

🔹 **Talc** is the softest mineral at point 1 on the hardness scale. One form of this mineral is called soapstone and can be easily carved into ornaments. It can be scratched with a fingernail.

🔹 **Diamond** is the hardest on the scale, at point 10. This highly prized gemstone is so hard that it is also used in industry as a cutting tool.

🔹 **The other minerals** on the scale are gypsum (2), calcite (3), fluorite (4), apatite (5), orthoclase (6), quartz (7), topaz (8), and corundum (9).

🔹 **Certain everyday objects** are also used for testing hardness. A fingernail (2½), coin (3½), and knife blade (5½) are often used.

DID YOU KNOW?

The first nine minerals on Mohs scale have roughly the same gap between them—that is, corundum is nine times harder than talc. Diamond, however, the tenth mineral on the scale, is 40 times harder than talc.

▼ *The ten-point hardness scale uses well-known minerals for its reference points.*

6	7	8	9	10
Orthoclase	Quartz	Topaz	Corundum	Diamond

Mineral colors

◈ **Minerals** range widely in colors, helping geologists tell them apart.

◈ **Mineral color** depends on how light is reflected and absorbed by the elements in the mineral.

◈ **Quartz**, a very common mineral, can occur in many different colors. Amethyst is purple, citrine is yellow, and the pink form is called rose quartz. Usually, quartz is gray or milky white.

◈ **Malachite**, which is a copper mineral, is a rich green color. Azurite, another mineral containing copper, is bright blue.

◈ **Common minerals** such as calcite, gypsum, and barite are usually white.

◈ **Minerals** that contain iron, such as hematite and magnetite, are often reddish-brown or black.

◀ Cinnabar is a bright-red mineral that contains mercury.

Gold is a rich yellow color. Fool's gold (pyrite) is a similar color, as is copper pyrite (chalcopyrite). It is easy to tell them apart using other tests such as hardness and specific gravity.

Cinnabar, a sulfide of mercury, is red, as is realgar (arsenic sulfide).

For thousands of years, mineral colors have been used as pigment in paints and dyes. Malachite was used as a green pigment more than 2,000 years ago in Egypt.

Ultramarine, a rich deep-blue color, is made from powdered lazurite (lapis lazuli).

▲ The brilliant green coating on this rock surface is the copper mineral conichalcite. Many minerals that contain copper are green.

Gemstones

Gemstones have been prized for thousands of years for their rarity, color, shape, and durability.

There are only a few dozen types of gemstone in everyday circulation. Other gemstones are too rare or soft to be of much use.

Semiprecious gemstones include many color varieties of quartz, such as purple amethyst.

Gemstones form naturally in many different geological situations. Some occur in igneous rocks, others in mineral veins or cavities.

▲ Small crystals of topaz. Topaz can be cut and facetted as gemstones.

Because of their hardness, gems such as ruby and sapphire are not worn away by erosion in a river and so accumulate in river gravels and sands. These forms of corundum have been weathered and eroded from their original source.

Diamond is the best-known gemstone. Imitation diamonds have been made for many years. Rock crystal (quartz) and glass have both been used, but today materials such as cubic zirconia are produced as diamond substitutes.

To enhance their natural beauty, and remove imperfections, gemstones are cut and surfaces called facets are made.

- **A person who** cuts and polishes gemstones is called a lapidary.

- **Gemstones**, especially diamonds, are measured in "carats." A carat is a measure of weight, being 0.2 grams.

▼ Each month of the year is characterized by a particular gemstone. The exact stones representing each month have not always been the same and those used in different countries vary. The stones here are those generally used today.

December Turquoise

January Garnet

November Topaz

February Amethyst

October Opal

March Aquamarine

September Sapphire

April Diamond

August Peridot

May Emerald

July Ruby

June Pearl

Precious metals

🔹 **Gold, silver, and platinum** are all minerals that are precious metals. They occur on their own as "native elements," which means they are not combined with other elements as compounds.

🔹 **Gold** is easily recognized by its rich color and great weight. It is 19 times heavier than an equal volume of water.

▲ Gold is often found in quartz veins. This fine crystal of quartz has small flakes of gold on its surfaces.

- **Gold is a soft metal**, easily scratched with a coin.

- **Found in a variety** of geological situations, gold occurs in veins, often with quartz. It occurs in river sand and shingle, where prospectors "pan for gold."

- **Native platinum metal** occurs as rare, silvery nuggets and minute grains with nickel and gold.

- **Platinum** commands a higher price on the world market than gold. It is used in catalytic converters, oil refining, and jewelry.

- **Silver** is far less valuable than gold or platinum. When clean, it has a fine metallic luster, but this rapidly fades and the metal becomes dull.

- **Silver** forms in delicate twisted wire shapes. Today, most silver is obtained from lead and copper mining and refining.

▲ This small specimen of silver is a mass of interlocking wires. It has become tarnished and has lost its bright metallic luster.

- **As well as being used** to make jewelry and ornaments, silver is a component of photographic film.

Mining

- **The metals and fuels** on which we depend are mined or quarried from the ground.

- **Rock** that contains valuable material, usually metal, is called an ore. Hematite is an iron ore and bauxite is an ore of aluminum.

- **More than 3,000 million tons** of metal and mineral ores are mined each year.

- **Ores are finite**, nonrenewable materials. It is therefore important to recycle metals after use.

- **Metal ores** exist in many different geological settings. How they are mined largely depends on the size and shape of the deposit.

- **If an ore body is large**, in rocks that are structurally strong, and occurs at depth, an underground mine will be used.

- **Surface (open pit) mining** is cheaper to carry out than underground mining. It can also produce far more ore in less time.

- **If the ore** is in loose surface sediments, it can be mined by using high-pressure water jets. Settling tanks may be used to separate the heavy ore from unwanted sand and clay.

◄ *Bauxite is an important ore of aluminum. This metal is strong and lightweight and doesn't rust like steel.*

▲ *Some of the world's biggest copper mines are in Chile. Miners remove the copper ore from mines or open pits on the surface.*

Coal mining was once a major industry in Britain, with hundreds of mines. Today, because of the low price of foreign coal and the use of other fuels, only a handful of mines are still working. Coal is also extracted by opencast methods.

Old mine workings and spoil heaps are excellent places to look for mineral specimens, if care is taken and permission sought from the landowner.

127

Crystals

🔹 **Many minerals** can form as crystals. These have surfaces that often join together perfectly.

🔹 **Crystals** show symmetry. As a crystal is turned round, the same shape may be seen a number of times.

🔹 **Mineralogists**, scientists who study minerals and crystals, classify crystals into a number of "systems," according to their symmetry. The most symmetrical crystal system is called the cubic system.

🔹 **Geologists** tell one type of mineral from another by using special tests. Many of these are easy to carry out.

🔹 **Not all minerals** that form within a certain system will have the same crystal shape. In the cubic system there can be many shapes, including cubes and octahedra (eight-sided crystals). These shapes share the same symmetry.

▼ *A fine group of small, reddish, six-sided vanadinite crystals.*

▲ Rhodochrosite often forms in banded masses. This specimen shows flat, tabular crystals.

◀ **The shape of a crystal** results from the way the atoms it is made of are fixed together.

◀ **Many rocks**, especially igneous rocks, are made of crystals of different minerals.

◀ **Some crystals** are transparent and allow light to pass completely through them.

◀ **The way the atoms** of a crystal are arranged may allow the crystal to break along a flat surface. This is called mineral cleavage.

◀ **Some crystals** break with a rough surface. This is known as mineral fracture.

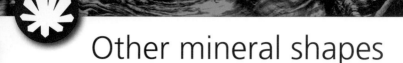

Other mineral shapes

- **The actual shape** in which a mineral forms is called its habit. This may be a perfect crystal shape or one of a number of other shapes.

- **Mineral habit** is a useful aid to help in identifying minerals.

- **When a mineral** forms no definite shape, it is said to have a massive habit. Lots of minerals, such as quartz and limonite (an old mineral), have this habit. They can also be crystalline.

- **Rounded habits** are common. Hematite (iron oxide) often occurs as reniform (kidney-shaped) masses.

- **A botryoidal habit** is like a bunch of grapes, with many small, rounded structures. Malachite can occur like this.

- **Native metallic elements**, such as silver and copper, frequently form as wires. These can look like tree branches and this habit is called dendritic (from the Greek word for a tree).

- **Minerals** sometimes form in elongated masses like stalactites. Goethite (an iron mineral) often has this stalactitic habit.

- **Well-formed crystals** that have a constant shape in cross-section are said to possess prismatic habit. A hexagonal quartz crystal is prismatic.

◄ *Marcasite has the same chemical composition as pyrite, but has different forms. This marcasite "sun" is a typical habit of the mineral.*

▶ *Native copper commonly occurs as twisted masses and wires.*

◀ **Mica crystals** are flat and flaky, rather like a table top. This habit is called tabular.

◀ **A habit** that looks like a fossil coral is called coralloidal. Aragonite (a form of calcium carbonate) sometimes occurs in this way.

▼ *This is not a fossil plant but delicate patterns formed by the mineral pyrolusite. This is known as dendritic habit.*

Mineral occurrence

Many of the finest mineral specimens and some of the rarest minerals are found in mineral veins.

▼ *A specimen of blue plumbogummite and yellowish pyromorphite. Countless tons of economically useful minerals come from veins.*

- **When rocks break** because of tension in the Earth's crust, faults and joints are formed. Hot fluids from great depths seep upward into these cracks and deposit minerals. These fractures become mineral veins.

- **Hot mineral-forming fluids** are called hydrothermal fluids because they are rich in water.

- **Minerals** containing important metals such as galena (lead), sphalerite (zinc), chalcopyrite (copper), and cassiterite (tin) occur in mineral veins.

- **Other common** hydrothermal vein minerals are fluorite, calcite, and quartz.

- **Hydrothermal veins** are often associated with large granite batholiths. Hot mineral-rich fluids may form after much of the magma has cooled.

- **Granite** is a rock through which heat rises for millions of years after it has crystallized. Fluids from elsewhere in the Earth's crust may be drawn upward by this heat and many deposit minerals near the granite.

- **A mineral vein** looks like a gash running through rocks. It is often white, containing quartz as the most common mineral.

- **Many minerals occur** in what are called placer deposits. These are concentrations of certain minerals in river sand and silt, especially where the water slows down on the inside of a meander or below rapids.

- **Only minerals** that are very durable and heavy are found in placers. Gold, tin, platinum, and diamonds occur in placers.

Quartz

- **One of the most common minerals** is quartz. It is widespread and occurs in most rocks.

- **Quartz** can be a great variety of colors. Some of the color forms are gemstones. Amethyst (purple), rose quartz (pink), smoky quartz (black and dark brown), and citrine (orange) are all cut and polished for jewelry.

- **Quartz** is the hardest common mineral. It is the defining mineral at point 7 on the hardness scale, and can't be scratched with a knife blade.

▲ Amethyst is the purple-colored form of quartz.

- **Agate**, a stone formed in concentric bands, has the same chemical composition as quartz.

- **Chalcedony** is a variety of quartz made of microscopic crystals.

DID YOU KNOW?

The largest quartz crystal ever discovered was found in Brazil. It was 20 ft long and weighed 53 tons.

- **Quartz** often occurs as magnificent crystals. These are six-sided (hexagonal) and usually have six triangular faces, forming a pyramid at the top.

- **Quartz** is made of atoms of silicon and oxygen in the form of silicon dioxide.

- **There are many** ways in which quartz is used. Small crystals of quartz are used in the mechanisms of watches and electronics equipment.

- **Colorless**, transparent quartz is called rock crystal.

▶ This is a hexagonal crystal of smoky quartz (Cairngorm). It is translucent and light is able to penetrate the crystal.

135

Spinel and rutile

◀ **Oxides are composed of metals** combined with oxygen. Spinel is an oxide of magnesium and aluminum and metals such as zinc, manganese, and iron. Rutile is an oxide of titanium dioxide.

◀ **Spinel forms** as octahedra. These are crystals with eight triangular faces, which form two four-sided pyramids joined at their bases.

◀ **It has a great variety of colors** and may be red, green, brown, black, or blue.

◀ **It can be produced artificially**, and these spinel specimens are slightly denser than natural ones.

◀ **It is an extremely hard mineral**, registering nearly point 8 on the hardness scale.

▼ *These worn spinel crystals are from river gravel in Burma. Because it is hard and resistant to erosion by running water, this mineral often occurs in river sediments.*

DID YOU KNOW?

Rutile is an important source of titanium, which is used in lightweight alloys in aircraft and artificial hip joints.

◄ *Inside this quartz crystal, thin needles of rutile can clearly be seen.*

🔹 **Spinel has been cut** as a gemstone, prized for its color and hardness.

🔹 **Rutile often occurs** as thin, needlelike crystals enclosed inside quartz crystals. It may also form as irregular masses.

🔹 **It is dark in color**, varying from red-brown to black.

🔹 **It is not as hard as spinel**, having a hardness of 6 to 6½.

Goethite

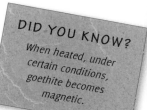

This mineral is named after the German writer Johann Wolfgang von Goethe (1749–1832), who was a mineral collector.

Goethite is rich in iron, and is mined as an ore of this metal. Chemically, it is iron hydroxide.

It is a dark-colored mineral. It can be black, dark brown, or yellowish brown.

The yellowish-colored material called limonite contains a lot of goethite. Some geologists regard limonite as a rock rather than a mineral because it contains various minerals.

◄ Goethite often occurs as small, grapelike aggregates. In this specimen, these can be seen in the lower left and upper center of the photograph.

- **It can form fine crystals,** but more frequently goethite occurs as rounded or irregular specimens.

- **This is a relatively hard mineral**—about the same as a knife blade at point 5 to 5½ on the hardness scale.

- **As it contains iron,** goethite is a dense mineral and specimens feel heavier than expected. Its density can be 4.3 times greater than that of water.

- **When light falls** on its surface, goethite has a different appearance depending on its shape. Crystals reflect the light with a sparkling sheen called an adamantine luster. Irregular specimens can look dull, with no sheen.

- **Goethite occurs** where iron-bearing deposits have been altered by oxidation and weathering.

▶ *Goethite can form thin, needlelike crystals, which are dark in color.*

Feldspar and mica

🔹 **The group of minerals** called feldspars are the most common minerals in the Earth's crust. Feldspars are generally pale colored, though some are reddish, bluish, or green.

🔹 **Feldspar** makes up nearly half the composition of basalt lava, which covers the floor of the oceans.

🔹 **Feldspar** is a silicate mineral containing silicon and oxygen. Different types of feldspar have atoms of different metallic elements.

🔹 **Orthoclase feldspar** is a silicate of potassium and aluminum. This is common in granite.

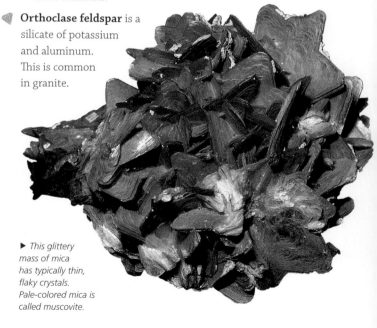

▶ This glittery mass of mica has typically thin, flaky crystals. Pale-colored mica is called muscovite.

- **Plagioclase feldspar** has a variable composition. It is a silicate of sodium and aluminum or calcium and aluminum. This feldspar mainly occurs in basalt and related rocks.

- **Feldspar** is used in pottery glazes and glass. It alters to china clay when decomposed.

- **Mica** is a complex silicate containing potassium, aluminum, and iron.

▶ Feldspar is a very common mineral and is commonly white or pale colored. Amazonite is a brilliant blue-green variety, seen here as fine crystals.

- **Because of its very glittery appearance** and flaky habit, mica is easy to identify.

- **Mica is common** in many igneous rocks, especially granite.

- **Mica has good** insulating properties and is often powdered and used for this purpose.

Augite and hornblende

- **A member of the mineral group** called pyroxenes, augite is a silicate formed at high temperatures in magma and lava.

- **Augite is a dark**, virtually black mineral that helps to give basic rocks their dark coloring. It can also be brown or dark green.

- **Augite crystals** are small, prismatic, and stubby.

- **Augite crystals** make up about 50 percent of gabbro, a coarse-grained igneous rock.

- **Hornblende** is very like augite in appearance. It belongs to the amphibole group of minerals.

◀ *This is a thin slice of hornblende gabbro, photographed through a microscope. The brightly colored, striped crystals are hornblende.*

▲ *A broken crystal of hornblende. Hornblende crystals tend to be longer than those of augite.*

▶ Augite crystals are usually short and stubby. When they break they display rectangular cross-sections.

- 🔹 **A very dark-colored** mineral, hornblende can be green, brown, or black.

- 🔹 **The crystals** formed by hornblende are long and prismatic, often with a fibrous appearance.

- 🔹 **Hornblende forms** in pale-colored igneous rocks such as granite and porphyry.

- 🔹 **The metamorphic rock** called amphibolite contains much hornblende.

- 🔹 **When hornblende and augite break**, different angles are produced between the cleavage. Hornblende breaks with an angle of either 60° or 120° between them. Augite breaks with 90° between the surfaces.

Olivine

- **Olivine crystallizes** at very high temperatures in basalts and related rocks.

- **It is a greenish** or brown mineral, which occurs as small grains or crystals.

- **The color of olivine** varies depending on its chemical composition. It is a silicate of iron and magnesium. An increase in iron content gives a browner color.

- **One of the hardest** rock-forming minerals, olivine is almost as hard as quartz.

- **Meteorites** found in Antarctica, belonging to a group called "stony-irons," are made of metal and the mineral olivine.

- **Because of its green color** and hardness, fine crystalline olivine is used as a gemstone called peridot.

◀ *In this specimen of basalt from Hawaii there is a mass of pale green olivine crystals.*

▲ *Olivine can be cut and facetted as a gem stone. This small cut stone is surrounded by water-worn olivine crystals. Gem-quality olivine is called peridot.*

- **Gem-quality olivine** comes mainly from Arizona, Myanmar (Burma), and Norway.

- **In basalt lava**, olivine occurs as bright-green, rounded crystals studding the rock surface.

- **Peridotite**, a rock which forms very deep in the Earth's crust, is composed of garnet and olivine.

- **Dunite** is an igneous rock made almost entirely of olivine. It has a greenish-brown appearance.

Actinolite and riebeckite

◀ **The mineral actinolite** is a complex silicate mineral that contains the metals calcium, magnesium, and iron.

◀ **It belongs to the family of minerals** called amphiboles. These are common in many igneous and metamorphic rocks.

◀ **This mineral is usually dark in color**—dark green to almost black. However, scratches on the surface are white.

◀ **It is relatively hard** at point 5 to 6 on the hardness scale, and may be marked by a steel knife blade.

▶ These are polished specimens of the mineral nephrite, which is a variety of actinolite.

- **It occurs mainly** in metamorphic rocks, especially schist and amphibolite.

- **Another complex silicate**, riebeckite forms as long, thin crystals.

- **This mineral is dark blue** to black in color, and the crystal surfaces have a silky sheen.

- **With a hardness of 5**, it can be scratched with a steel knife blade.

- **Fibrous riebeckite** (crocidolite) has asbestoslike properties, which is why it is known as "blue asbestos." It has been used for heat and electrical insulation.

▶ *This riebeckite shows a silky luster. It is composed of many slender, fibrous crystals. This form is known as crocidolite.*

Galena and cassiterite

- **Galena** (lead sulfide) has been mined since Roman times as an ore of lead.

- **A very dense mineral**, galena is made of lead sulfide, and is 7.5 times heavier than an equal volume of water.

- **Galena** is a soft, gray-colored mineral, easily scratched with a coin. It crystallizes in the cubic system and is often found as near perfect cubes.

- **Lead** was once used to make water and gas pipes because it was easily bent to the correct shape. However, it fractures and produces a cumulative poison that builds up in the body.

▲ Galena is a heavy, metallic, lead-gray mineral. It occurs in mineral veins with quartz, fluorite, and calcite.

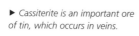

▶ Cassiterite is an important ore of tin, which occurs in veins.

- **For thousands of years** the county of Cornwall in the UK was a source of tin, extracted from cassiterite (tin oxide).

- **This mineral** occurs in hydrothermal veins, often associated with large granite batholiths.

- **Cassiterite** can be recognized by its dark brown or black color and high density. It is a hard mineral—even a knife blade will not scratch it.

- **About 5,000 years ago**, the Mesopotamians made bronze by adding tin to copper.

- **Pewter**, used much in the past for drinking vessels, is an alloy of tin and lead. Tin is used today in solder and tin plate.

- **Today, lead is used** in vehicle batteries and as a shield against radioactive sources.

▶ Today, one of the main uses of lead is for the plates in vehicle batteries. Lead is obtained from galena.

Chalcocite and bornite

◀ **These two minerals** are common sulfides of copper. Bornite also contains iron.

◀ **Both chalcocite and bornite** are important ores that are mined for their copper content.

Chalcocite forms in the same mineral veins as bornite, along with other minerals such as galena and sphalerite.

It rarely forms crystals. It usually occurs as shapeless masses.

It is a dark-gray mineral, and shines like metal when light falls on its surface.

A soft mineral, chalcocite can be easily scratched by a coin, having a hardness of point 2½ to 3 on the hardness scale.

Bornite forms in fine, cube-shaped crystals, and also in eight- or twelve-sided crystals.

This mineral can be a variety of colors, indicating its copper and iron content. It can be copper-red, bronze, or brown.

For an ore of a metal, bornite is a soft mineral, and can be marked by a coin. Its hardness is 3.

◄ *This specimen has some pale masses of quartz among the purple-tarnished bornite. It is from Cumbria, UK, where, many years ago, copper was mined.*

Cinnabar

- **This mineral** is bright red or occasionally a brownish color.

- **It forms around volcanic craters** and hot springs, and in fractures in sedimentary rocks.

- **Cinnabar is usually found** as shapeless masses, but it can form as fine, six-sided crystals.

- **It is a soft mineral** that is easily marked by a coin.

- **It occurs with other minerals**, including pyrite, realgar, quartz, and calcite.

- **Cinnabar is the main source** of the metal mercury, which is extracted by heating.

- **Mercury is a poisonous metal**, and cinnabar should be handled with care.

- **It is heavy and dense** at more than eight times as dense as water.

▶ Cinnabar can form as six-sided crystals, but is usually found as irregular masses (shown here).

◀ **Mercury is a heavy liquid** at ordinary temperatures, and has been used in thermometers and dental fillings.

◀ **As well as occurring in cinnabar,** mercury is widespread throughout the natural world. It is found in corderoite and other minerals, but is poisonous to most animals and plants.

▶ *In Asia, ornamental pieces such as this vase are often made of cinnabar.*

153

Arsenopyrite and marcasite

- **The mineral arsenopyrite** is a sulfide of iron and arsenic. Marcasite is a form of iron sulfide.

- **Arsenopyrite occurs** as elongated crystals, and also as grains and irregular masses.

▼ This elongated mass of globular marcasite is from the chalk of southern England, UK. Marcasite is often found in sedimentary rocks.

- **It is a relatively hard mineral**, about the same hardness as a steel knife blade. Its density is around six times that of water.

- **This mineral is silvery-gray** in color, but tarnishes to brown and pink.

- **Arsenic can be sourced** from arsenopyrite, and the use of this poisonous element is controlled.

- **It forms in mineral veins** with other minerals including quartz and calcite, and in silver- and gold-bearing deposits.

- **Pyrite is chemically the same** as marcasite, but the crystal forms of the two are very different.

- **This form of iron sulfide** occurs in a variety of shapes, often with curved crystal faces. Nodules (rounded lumps) of marcasite have radiating internal structures.

- **It is paler in color** than pyrite and is brassy yellow, but gets darker after prolonged exposure in the atmosphere.

DID YOU KNOW?
When arsenopyrite is struck with a hard object, a smell of garlic is produced.

Iron ores

🔹 **Iron** is one of the most sought-after raw materials.

🔹 **Many** of the sedimentary iron ores of the Jurassic age in England, UK, are now composed of rusty-colored limonite. This resulted from the weathering of other iron minerals and concentrated the iron into sufficient quantities to make it workable. In the fresh state, many of these ores were not economic to work.

▶ *This 2,000-year-old iron chain was found in a Welsh Lake called Llyn Cerrig Bach.*

🔹 **Most iron ore** mined today is found in sedimentary rocks. The richest deposits are in Labrador (Canada), Hamersley (Western Australia), near Lake Superior, and in the Ukraine.

🔹 **Hematite (iron oxide)** is a rich ore. It is a mineral with either a black or a reddish color.

🔹 **Hematite** frequently occurs in rounded, "kidney ore" shapes. The crystalline form is called specularite.

- **As it contains iron**, hematite is a heavy mineral with a specific gravity 5.26 times heavier than water.

- **Magnetite** is another rich source of iron. This oxide of iron forms as black crystals or massive, irregular specimens.

- **As its name suggests**, magnetite is magnetic. This magnetism is strong enough to move a compass needle and attract iron filings.

- **Mountaineers and walkers** in areas where the rocks contain magnetite will find their compasses give inaccurate readings.

- **Magnetite** is a hard mineral and can't be scratched by a knife blade.

- **In Tenerife** in the Canary Islands, there are black magnetite sand beaches, made of iron ore that has been weathered out of lava.

▼ *Two different varieties of hematite are seen in this specimen—reddish, rounded kidney ore and black, crystalline specularite.*

Bauxite

◀ **Some geologists** argue that bauxite is a rock, not a mineral, because it is a mixture of various materials. These include several oxides of aluminum.

◀ **Bauxite is usually formed** by the weathering of other rocks rich in silicates of aluminum. This happens mainly in tropical regions.

◀ **It is an attractive material**, being orange or buff-colored and containing red specks and patches.

◀ **As well as aluminum**, bauxite commonly contains some iron oxide.

▲ *Bauxite is a dull, red-brown ore of aluminum. This is the most abundant of all metals and much electrical energy is needed to extract it from bauxite.*

▲ Aluminum is very strong and lightweight, so it is suitable for aircraft construction. Unlike steel, it does not rust.

- **Bauxite** is a very soft material, easily scratched with a fingernail. It is also low density and is only 2.5 times heavier than water.

- **Much mined** for its aluminum content, bauxite is the major source of this metal.

- **Aluminum** conducts electricity well and is lightweight.

- **It is obtained** from its ore by electrolysis. This involves the use of much electricity, which is often low-cost hydroelectricity.

- **Aluminum** is very resistant to corrosion. It does not rust like iron and steel.

- **Because of its strength** and light weight, aluminum is used in the construction industry and increasingly in vehicle manufacture.

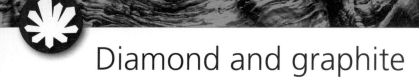

Diamond and graphite

- **Diamond and graphite** are remarkably different forms of the same element, carbon. The properties of these two forms of carbon result from the way their atoms are joined.

- **Many diamonds** may be more than 3,000 million years old.

- **Graphite** is very soft, being easily scratched with a fingernail.

- **Diamond** forms small, glassy, often octahedral crystals in the cubic crystal system and is the hardest known mineral.

DID YOU KNOW?
Many diamonds were formed at a depth of 125 mi.

▶ Diamond has been prized as a gemstone for thousands of years. This example has been cut and facetted to show off its sparkle.

◀ This diamond–bearing rock formed deep in the Earth and was carried upward by an erupting volcano.

Graphite forms in flat, platelike pieces with a six-sided outline (hexagonal crystal system). These have a dull, greasy, or metallic sheen.

The atoms in diamond are joined in groups of five. These link together in a tight, close structure.

In graphite, the atoms are arranged in layers or sheets that are weakly joined.

Diamond is much prized as a gemstone and is also used for industrial cutting.

Graphite is used as pencil "lead." The pencil industry in Keswick, UK, was based on local graphite.

▶ The "lead" in pencils is made from graphite because it is soft.

Beryl and tourmaline

- **These two minerals** are both silicates of various metals. They occur in igneous rocks such as granites and pegmatites.

- **Beryl** is harder than quartz and forms fine, hexagonal crystals.

- **A number** of color varieties of beryl are known, many of which are gemstones. Emerald is the rich-green variety of beryl, heliodor is yellow, morganite is a pink form, and aquamarine is greenish-blue.

- **Beryl can be translucent** or transparent, and has a glassy luster (sheen).

- **Tourmaline** is not uncommon in granites, where it forms black prismatic crystals. This type of tourmaline is called schorl.

▲ *Some of the color varieties of tourmaline.*

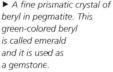

DID YOU KNOW?

The largest crystal ever found was a beryl crystal discovered in Madagascar in 1976. It was 60 ft long and weighed 420 tons.

◀ **With a hardness of 7**, tourmaline is as hard as quartz. It forms prismatic crystals and may be transparent.

◀ **There are more** color varieties of tourmaline than of any other gemstone.

◀ **Rubellite** is a pink tourmaline, and the green form is called elbaite. It can also be blue, yellowish, and gray-blue.

◀ **Some tourmaline crystals** are green at one end and pink at the other.

▶ *A fine prismatic crystal of beryl in pegmatite. This green-colored beryl is called emerald and it is used as a gemstone.*

Opal

Opal is a form of silicon dioxide, but is chemically different from quartz because it also contains water in its structure.

The silica in opal is packed together in minute spheres. Opal is thus a noncrystalline mineral.

Opal occurs in many different forms. It can be botryoidal (shaped like a bunch of grapes), reniform (kidney-shaped), or shaped like a stalactite.

Opal is a well-known gemstone, though it is not of great hardness. Nevertheless, it has a number of attractive features.

Because of the packing of minute spheres in the structure of opal, light is scattered to produce many colors. These vary from blue and green to red and pink. When heated, opal may change color.

▶ Opal is often used in jewelry because of its striking colors.

▶ This Australian opal shows typical color variation from green to blue. Being translucent, light passes into the mineral and gives the colors depth.

- **Another feature** of gem opal is the way it produces flashes of color, which are best shown in curved, polished specimens called cabochons.

- **Opal** forms in certain volcanic rocks, but also often around hot springs.

- **The Romans** considered opal to be a symbol of power and the Aztec civilization valued it as a gem.

- **Today**, much of the world's opal comes from Australia, but some also comes from Mexico.

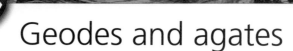

Geodes and agates

- **A geode** is a gas cavity (vesicle) in lava, usually basalt, which has been filled in with minerals. Quartz in various forms is common in geodes.

- **Basalt lava** erupts onto the Earth's surface at over 1,800°F. As it cools, gas is released and small cavities are left where the gas bubbles were trapped.

- **When basalt** containing geodes is weathered, the geodes, being very hard, are left behind. They often look like lumpy potatoes, but when cut open, the colored bands of agate are revealed.

▲ This sliced geode has a hollow in its center with crystals growing into it, surrounded by bands of agate.

▶ *This agate shows typical alternating color bands. The specimen has been cut and polished.*

- **In some geodes**, agate lines the cavity and delicate crystals grow into the hollow interior.

- **Agate** is not made of crystalline quartz. In an agate, the quartz is in minute fibers and grains.

- **Agate** is one of the most varied semiprecious stones. It occurs in many forms and colors.

- **A hard gemstone**, agate is translucent, and can be gray, blue, red, green, white, or other colors.

- **Agate** often occurs in bands of different colors. These may be parallel (onyx) or concentric.

- **South American agates** from Uruguay and Brazil are the most common.

- **In Britain**, agates can be found in many places. Southern Scotland is the source of the best British agates. They also occur in the Cheviot Hills in Northumberland, in Cornwall, and on North Sea beaches.

Native raw elements

- **As well as gold and diamond**, there are a number of other minerals that are important native elements.

- **Copper** is a metal that occurs as dendritic and shapeless, massive specimens. It is soft and easily scratched, but is very dense.

- **Copper** also combines with other elements in various minerals. One of its main uses is in electrical wiring.

- **Arsenic** usually occurs as rounded, botryoidal masses and can also be found in the form of grains.

- **A group of minerals** called arsenates contain arsenic combined with other elements. Arsenic is poisonous.

- **Sulfur** is a bright-yellow element that can occur as fine pyramidal crystals.

- **Sulfur** forms around hot springs and volcanic craters. It often combines with other elements to form the sulfide group of minerals.

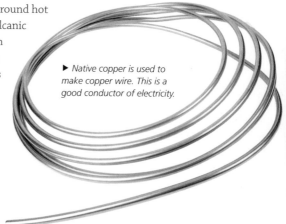

▶ Native copper is used to make copper wire. This is a good conductor of electricity.

▼ *Sulfur's crystals are clearly visible and are a bright yellow color. This specimen is from Mexico. Sulfur has important industrial uses, especially in the manufacture of sulfuric acid.*

🔹 **The element bismuth**, a silvery, metallic mineral that is soft but very dense, occurs in hydrothermal veins and pegmatites.

🔹 **Bismuth** also occurs combined with sulfur as a mineral called bismuthinite.

DID YOU KNOW?
Copper pins and beads have been discovered in the Middle East, dating back more than 7,000 years.

Radioactive minerals

⬤ **There are a few minerals** that contain uranium, a dense, radioactive element.

⬤ **Uranium** combines with oxygen to form uraninite (pitchblende), with copper, phosphorus, and oxygen to form torbernite. It also combines with calcium, phosphorus, and oxygen to make autunite.

⬤ **Uranium** is sought after as a source of fuel for nuclear reactors. Other highly radioactive elements, such as plutonium, can be made from it.

⬤ **Torbernite** forms as bright green, box-shaped crystals. These have a shiny surface.

◄ *In 1898, the Polish scientist Marie Curie (shown here with her daughter) and her French husband Pierre discovered radioactivity. They identified the elements radium, potassium, and helium in a specimen of uraninite.*

- **Easily scratched** with a coin, torbernite forms by the alteration of uraninite by fluids in the Earth's crust.

- **Autunite** is bright yellow or green and occurs as small crystals and crusty masses.

- **Like torbernite** autunite is easily scratched with a coin and is only of average density.

- **Radioactive minerals** are only for expert use. They have to be stored securely, often in lead-lined containers.

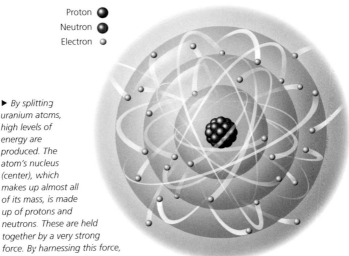

Proton
Neutron
Electron

▶ By splitting uranium atoms, high levels of energy are produced. The atom's nucleus (center), which makes up almost all of its mass, is made up of protons and neutrons. These are held together by a very strong force. By harnessing this force, nuclear energy is made.

Wavellite and turquoise

⬩ **Both these minerals have complex**, but similar, chemical compositions. Wavellite is a hydrated aluminum phosphate. Turquoise is a hydrated phosphate of copper and aluminum.

⬩ **Wavellite is well known** for its radiating crystal aggregates. These form in rounded masses, with an internal radiating structure.

▲ *Turquoise is soft and can be shaped and polished easily. Small, rounded pieces have been joined to make this colorful necklace.*

▶ When rounded masses of wavellite are broken, their internal structure of radiating crystals can be seen. The specimen at the top left of the picture shows this well.

◀ **This mineral varies in color** from green to yellow, with a pearly or glassy sheen.

◀ **It is slightly harder than a coin**, at 3½ to 4, and has a low density of 2.36.

◀ **It occurs in mineral veins** and on fractures in rocks that fluids have moved through.

◀ **Turquoise is known** for its decorative uses, in both jewelry and ornaments.

◀ **Its main feature** is its bright-blue color. It may also be green or gray.

◀ **It usually occurs** as irregular masses and crusts on rock surfaces. It rarely forms as small crystals.

◀ **Another important feature** in minerals that are used for jewelry is hardness. Although not of great hardness, turquoise resists some scratching at hardness 5 to 6.

◀ **Turquoise forms** in rocks rich in aluminum that have been altered by ground water.

Fool's gold

◆ **There are a number** of minerals that on first sight have the appearance of gold. Small golden flecks of mineral in a stream bed may catch the eye but after testing are found not to be the real thing.

◆ **The two minerals** generally referred to as fool's gold are pyrite (iron sulfide) and chalcopyrite (copper iron sulfide).

◆ **With a few simple tests**, it is very easy to tell real gold from other minerals, and not be fooled.

◆ **Pyrite** is a common mineral in many geological situations. It occurs in mineral veins, metamorphic and sedimentary rocks, and in some igneous rocks. Fossils are often preserved in pyrite.

◆ **The true color** of pyrite is silvery yellow, not a rich deep yellow like gold.

▶ Pyrite commonly occurs as fine, cube-shaped crystals with striations (lines) on their faces (as shown here).

◀ *Chalcopyrite is a richer yellow color than pyrite. It is also less hard and can be scratched with a knife blade.*

● **Gold** is a very soft mineral, which can be scratched with a coin, but pyrite is harder than a knife blade

● **Chalcopyrite** is a deeper yellow than pyrite and nearer to gold in color. However, chalcopyrite tarnishes on exposure to air to give wonderful "peacock" colors.

● **Chalcopyrite** is softer than pyrite, but harder than gold.

● **Both types** of fool's gold are not nearly as dense as near true gold. An equal-sized specimen of gold would be far heavier than the impostors.

● **Chalcopyrite** is a valuable mineral, being a very important ore of copper.

Halite and gypsum

◈ **These minerals** are both evaporites, formed by the drying up of salt lakes and shallow seas. Halite is a chloride and gypsum is a sulfate.

◈ **Both minerals** are of considerable economic importance, being used in the chemical and construction industries.

◈ **Gypsum** (hydrated calcium sulfate) is the basis for the manufacture of plaster and plasterboard. It is also used in cement manufacture.

◈ **Halite** (sodium chloride) is used in the manufacture of soap, dyes, caustic soda, insecticides, and chlorine. It is also used for deicing roads.

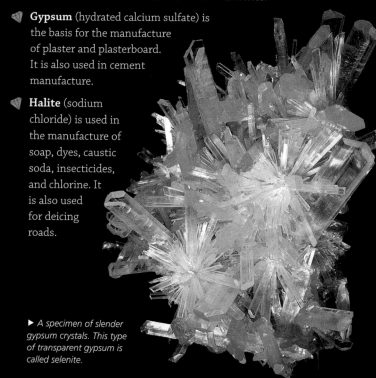

▶ *A specimen of slender gypsum crystals. This type of transparent gypsum is called selenite.*

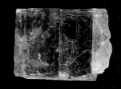

▶ Halite can form as cube-shaped crystals. These examples are transparent.

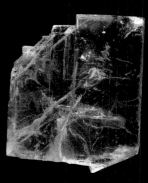

🔰 **Large chemical industries** are sited in England, UK, and Germany, where concentrations of salt (halite) occurs.

🔰 **Halite** can be readily identified by its salty taste. It is usually orange, gray, or white in color, but can be black.

🔰 **Because it is very soluble**, the cube-shaped crystals tend to lose their sharp edges unless they are kept in sealed, dry containers.

🔰 **Halite** is very soft, and easily scratched with a fingernail.

🔰 **Gypsum** often occurs as fine crystals. These can be diamond shaped or long and thin. A form called "daisy gypsum" is like a rosette of tiny flowers.

🔰 **Gypsum** is the definition of point 2 on the mineral hardness scale.

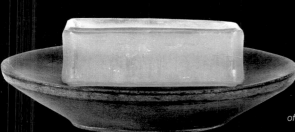

◀ One of the uses of halite is in the manufacture of soap.

Anhydrite

🔹 **This mineral is important** in the chemical industry. For many years it has been extracted for use in the production of sulfuric acid, fertilizers, and insecticides.

🔹 **Chemically, it is calcium sulfate.** Anhydrite is very similar to gypsum, but lacks gypsum's water molecules.

🔹 **Anhydrite can change** to gypsum in moist conditions.

▼ *This pale blue specimen of anhydrite shows a mass of flattened, prismatic crystals.*

- **It rarely forms crystals**. Usually it is found as irregular masses or fibers.

- **It is a pale-colored mineral**, commonly gray, white, or brownish. Some delicate blue and green specimens occur.

- **It can be told apart from gypsum** by its greater hardness. Anhydrite can just be marked by a coin, whereas gypsum is easily scratched by a fingernail.

- **Anhydrite has an average density** for minerals, and is 2.98 times denser than water.

- **This mineral usually occurs** as an evaporite. It forms with a number of other minerals when lakes, and especially salt water lagoons, dry up, and salts that have been dissolved in the water crystallize.

- **Anhydrite is also found** where rocks containing gypsum have been altered, for example, by metamorphism.

- **Minerals occurring with anhydrite** include halite, calcite, gypsum, and sylvine.

Calcite and rhodochrosite

◈ **Calcite and rhodochrosite** are both carbonate minerals. They are made of a metal joined in a chemical compound with carbon and oxygen.

◈ **Calcite** (calcium carbonate) is one of the most common minerals. It is the main mineral in limestone, and metamorphic marbles are composed of calcite.

◈ **Hydrothermal veins** often contain calcite along with other minerals, such as galena, sphalerite, and barite.

◈ **Calcite** is uncommon in igneous rocks. A group of volcanic and magmatic rocks called carbonatites are rich in carbonates. These are rare rocks usually found with syenite.

◈ **Calcite** defines point 3 on the hardness scale. It forms as sharply pointed or flattened six-sided crystals.

▲ *When calcite crystals have flattened tops thay are called nail-head crystals.*

◀ *This type of rhodochrosite, with different colored bands running through it, is often cut and polished ornamentally.*

Rhodochrosite (manganese carbonate) is a rich, deep pinkish-red color. Many minerals containing manganese are red.

Rhodochrosite can form as crystals, but also occurs in rounded or nodular masses.

Both calcite and rhodochrosite dissolve in hydrochloric acid (the acid needs to be warm to react with rhodochrosite). The bubbles given off are carbon dioxide.

Rhodochrosite occurs in hydrothermal veins and where rocks rich in manganese have been altered.

Because of its attractive color, rhodochrosite is cut and polished ornamentally.

Siderite and dolomite

🔹 **These two minerals have** a number of similarities, but are easily told apart by other properties. Chemically, they are both carbonates.

🔹 **Siderite is a carbonate** of iron. It is a chemical compound of iron, carbon, and oxygen. The carbon and oxygen together form the "carbonate" part of the formula.

🔹 **Dolomite is a carbonate of calcium** and magnesium. The word dolomite is also used as a rock name for the type of limestone that contains a high proportion of this mineral.

🔹 **A similarity between these two minerals** is that their crystal faces are often curved.

▲ Dolomite is white, cream, pink, or brown in color.

🔹 **Siderite is harder than a coin** but softer than a knife blade. Its hardness is 4. Its iron content gives it a density of about 4 times that of water.

🔹 **This mineral is usually a dull color**—gray, brown, black, or red are typical.

🔹 **Both these minerals** occur in mineral veins and in sedimentary rocks.

Softer than siderite, dolomite's hardness is about the same as that of a coin, at 3½ to 4. It has a density 2.85 times that of water, so is lighter than a same-sized specimen of siderite.

Dolomite will dissolve in cold, weak hydrochloric acid. It does not produce the violent effervescence that calcite does.

▼ *In this specimen from a mineral vein in Durham, UK, siderite occurs as grayish crystals. The white and colorless transparent crystals are quartz.*

183

Ulexite

- **Classified as a borate**, ulexite contains sodium, calcium, boron, and oxygen, joined in a chemical compound to molecules of water.

- **This mineral has been used** as an ore of boron. Compounds of this element are used to toughen glass, and in microchips and paper-making.

- **It often occurs as rounded masses**, but long, fibrous aggregates or fluffy-looking lumps called "cotton balls" made of many thin crystals are also found.

- **Ulexite is very soft.** It can be marked easily with a coin and sometimes by a fingernail.

▼ *When lakes dry out in arid regions, a variety of minerals can form as the water evaporates. Ulexite is an evaporite mineral formed in this situation.*

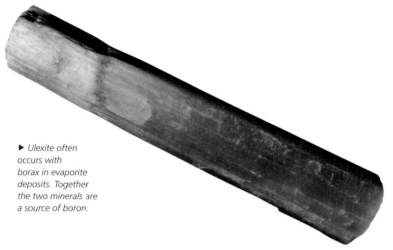

▶ *Ulexite often occurs with borax in evaporite deposits. Together the two minerals are a source of boron.*

- **This mineral has very low density**— only twice the density of water.

- **Masses of ulexite** are pale in color, usually white or colorless, with a silky sheen on the surface.

- **Many crystals of ulexite** are transparent, allowing light to pass through them.

- **A special property** of this mineral is that it can dissolve in hot water.

- **Ulexite forms** during the evaporation and drying out of lakes in desert regions, such as the Californian Desert.

DID YOU KNOW?

Crystal masses of ulexite have fiber optical properties. If these masses are polished at their ends, light and images can be transmitted along the crystals, giving it the alternative name "television stone."

Strange mineral properties

- **Because of their chemistry** or crystal structure, a number of minerals have properties that are special to them, and by which they can be readily identified.

- **A transparent crystal** of calcite is called Iceland spar. When an object is seen through such a crystal, it appears double. This is called double refraction.

- **Many minerals** react with acids. It is best only to test them with weak hydrochloric acid. Certain sulfides, such as galena, release hydrogen sulfide gas when reacting with this acid.

◀ Iceland spar is remarkable because it shows double refraction— objects seen through a crystal appear double.

◀ *Magnetite, as its name suggests, is magnetic. This specimen has attracted a paper clip.*

Certain minerals that contain iron are magnetic. Magnetite attracts iron filings. Hematite becomes magnetic when it is heated.

Ruby, sapphire, and some other minerals contain minute crisscross needles of rutile that produce a shining star shape when light shines on them. This optical property is known as asterism.

Quartz, tourmaline, and hemimorphite all develop electrical potential when subjected to mechanical stress.

Talc and molybdenite are flexible and can be bent. Mica, if bent, is flexible and reverts to its original shape.

When a mineral has a high-temperature flame directed onto it, the colors produced are related to the mineral's chemistry. Sodium minerals color the flame yellow, potassium gives a violet flame, and copper colors the flame green.

Halite, nitrate minerals, and some sulfates are soluble in water. Specimens of these have to be carefully stored.

Barite and celestite

- **Barite and celestite** are both sulfates. Barite contains the metal barium and celestite contains strontium.

- **They can both occur in** hydrothermal veins with a range of minerals, including quartz, galena, sphalerite, calcite, and dolomite.

- **Barite** may occur around hot springs and in nodules in clay. Celestite can be found in evaporite deposits and hydrothermal veins.

- **Barite is usually pale colored** and can be white, colorless and transparent, pink, brown, or gray. Fine crystals of barite are common and it also forms rounded masses called cockscomb barite.

- **Because it contains barium**, barite is a dense mineral. It weighs 4.5 times as much as an equal volume of water. This property helps to tell barite from other common pale-colored vein minerals.

- **Barite** is the main ore of barium metal. It is used in "drilling mud," a lubricant employed when drilling for oil.

▼ A group of delicate blue celestite crystals. This mineral is an ore of strontium.

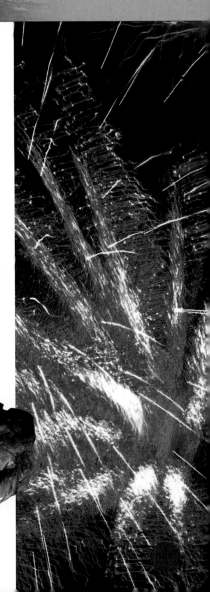

▶ The element strontium, which occurs in celestite, is used in fireworks. Strontium gives burning fireworks a rich-red color.

- **Celestite** can be colorless, gray, white, blue, or green and often forms shiny crystals, like those of barite.

- **Celestite** fluoresces under ultraviolet light, and is slightly soluble in water.

- **Strontium** is used in the manufacture of paint, car batteries, fireworks, glass, and flares.

▼ Some of these barite crystals have been colored by iron-rich fluids. Barite is one of the densest minerals found in mineral veins.

Kyanite and garnet

🔸 **Many minerals** develop during metamorphism. Two of the most attractive are kyanite and garnet.

🔸 **Kyanite** forms in rocks that have been regionally metamorphosed under conditions of considerable pressure and temperature.

🔸 **Schist and gneiss** are the rocks in which kyanite usually occurs.

🔸 **Kyanite** is often various shades of blue but may also be pink, green, gray, or yellow.

🔸 **In schist and gneiss**, kyanite occurs as long, thin, bladed crystals.

🔸 **An interesting feature** of kyanite is its varying hardness. This ranges between 4 and 7, depending on the direction in which it is scratched.

◀ *This fine mass of blue, blade-shaped kyanite crystals is from Brazil.*

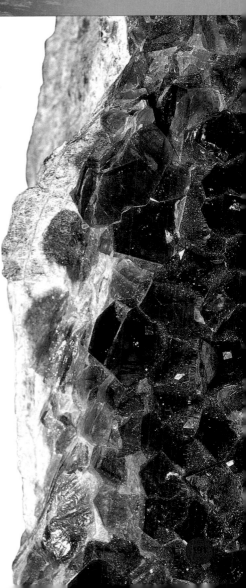

▶ There are many different named types of garnet. This red-brown variety is called grossular.

- **Garnet** is really the name for a family of minerals. Each garnet has slightly different chemical properties.

- **Garnet commonly forms as crystals** in the cubic system. The crystals are rarely simple cubes, but more usually complex shapes with parallelogram faces.

- **Garnets** can be dark red-brown, green, orange, or red.

- **Because it is harder** than quartz and has attractive colors, garnet is used as a gemstone.

Malachite and azurite

- **Malachite and azurite** have been prized since the Bronze Age for their colors. The two minerals often occur together in mineral veins.

- **Both malachite and azurite** are copper-bearing minerals. They are copper carbonates.

- **Where copper veins** have been altered by weathering and contact with fluids, malachite and azurite may be found.

- **A useful test** for both minerals is applying dilute, cold hydrochloric acid to them. A chemical reaction will occur, producing bubbles of carbon dioxide.

- **Malachite** is a brilliant deep-green color, and has been used as a paint pigment for more than 3,000 years.

▶ *Malachite is very soft, so it is easily cut and polished for jewelry and ornaments.*

▲ *Small crystals of deep-blue azurite coat this rock surface.*

◀ **As it is a soft mineral** (hardness 4), malachite can be easily shaped and polished ornamentally.

◀ **Malachite** often forms in rounded, botryoidal masses. When cut and polished, curved patterns can appear.

◀ **Azurite** is a rich, deep-blue color. This mineral has also been exploited as paint pigment for thousands of years.

◀ **Azurite occurs** in rounded masses and also as short, stocky crystals.

◀ **With a hardness** of only 4, azurite can be easily scratched with a knife.

Fluorite

- **Fluorite** is a common mineral in hydrothermal veins, where it occurs with galena, calcite, quartz, borite, and sphalerite.

- **Because of its chemical composition**, fluorite (calcium fluoride) has some important uses. It is used in the manufacture of hydrofluoric acid and the fluorine chemicals.

- **Fluorite forms cubic** and octahedral crystals. Perfect lenses can be manufactured from fluorite crystals.

- **In the iron** and steel industry, fluorite is used as a flux. This is a material added to the molten metal to take out impurities and form the slag.

- **In the past**, fluorite was often discarded when mineral veins were mined for lead and zinc. For this reason fine specimens can be found on old mine dumps.

▼ *These pale-green, cubic crystals of fluorite are transparent, allowing light to pass through them.*

▲ As well as forming fine crystals, fluorite also occurs in bands of different colors. This polished specimen from China has a thin layer of pyrite on its surface.

DID YOU KNOW?
Fluorite is sometimes cut and facetted as an imitation diamond.

🔻 **Fluorite** is the defining mineral at point 4 on the hardness scale.

🔻 **An attractive banded form** of fluorite, found in Derbyshire, UK, is called Blue John. This is cut and polished ornamentally.

🔻 **Fluorite** is commonly purple, green, or yellowish and the crystals are transparent.

🔻 **Often fluorite crystals** interlock. This property is called twinning. When seen in ultraviolet light, fluorite is strongly fluorescent.

Zeolite minerals

- **Zeolites** usually occur in the gas bubble hollows, called vesicles, in lavas. These hollows are left as the lava cools and gas escapes.

- **They are a group** of silicate minerals that have molecules of water in their chemical structure.

- **These minerals** form when hot water and other fluids seep through lava that has been cool for some time and buried in the Earth's crust.

- **Amygdales** are the infilled gas bubble cavities in lava. Amygdales can be made of quartz and agate as well as zeolite.

- **They have an open crystal structure**, rather like a miniature sieve. For this reason, zeolites are used to soak up moisture in industrial processes.

- **Most zeolites** are pale colored. They usually form good crystals, often in a mass of thin, radiating shapes.

- **Zeolites** often occur in concentric zones in thick lava flows.

- **Stilbite** is an unusual zeolite, as the crystals are in sheaflike aggregates.

- **Zeolites are also used** as water softeners, as they are able to exchange ions. The sodium-rich zeolite called natrolite will take calcium out of hard water by exchanging its sodium for calcium.

◄ This specimen shows fine crystals of the zeolite mineral, stilbite, growing into a cavity in basalt lava. The crystals are less than half an inch long.

Sapphire and ruby

🔹 **Corundum** is aluminum oxide and is the second-hardest mineral to diamond.

🔹 **Usually**, corundum forms as six-sided (hexagonal) crystals with pyramids at the top and bottom.

🔹 **Corundum** can occur in many colors, including pink, yellow, gray, green, and brown. Bright-red corundum is ruby and blue corundum is sapphire.

🔹 **Because of its great hardness** and rich colors, corundum is much valued as a gemstone.

🔹 **Corundum** forms in igneous and metamorphic rocks, but most of the gem quality stones are found in river shingle. This is an example of a placer deposit, where hard resistant minerals have been redeposited after erosion and transport.

🔹 **Famous sources** of gem corundum are Sri Lanka, Kashmir, Australia, Thailand, and eastern Africa.

🔹 **Certain rubies** are called star rubies. These show asterism, as small needles of rutile make a star effect in the ruby.

▲ *Sapphire is a form of corundum. Some people believe that it has healing and soothing properties.*

- **Corundum** is used as an abrasive. Emery is an impure form of corundum that often also contains iron minerals.

- **Corundum can be made** artificially. August Verneuil perfected the technique as long ago as 1900.

DID YOU KNOW?
Corundum crystals weighing 375 lb have been found in South Africa.

▼ These ruby crystals from India are in a specimen of metamorphic rock called gneiss. The pale crystals are quartz

Decorative noncrystalline minerals

- **Many minerals** that are noncrystalline have great value as ornamental stones, usually because of their colors.

- **The deep blue** lapis lazuli is mainly composed of lazurite. The finest material comes from Afghanistan. Russia and China are other sources.

- **Lazurite** contains veins of white calcite and pyrite. It is about as hard as a knife blade (hardness 5), and is translucent. Lapis is much used for jewelry.

▲ *Artists and jewelers have long prized the intense blue made from the lapis lazuli.*

- **Turquoise** is another blue, decorative mineral, though it is generally paler than lapis lazuli.

- **Turquoise can be green** if it contains much iron. Its blue color comes from a high copper content.

- **Much of the attractiveness** of turquoise lies in the veins of darker material that often run through it.

- **Jade** is the name given to the ornamental form of the minerals jadeite and nephrite.

▲ Because of its brilliant blue coloring, turquoise is often used ornamentally. These small specimens have been polished to show off their colors.

Jadeite and nephrite are as hard as quartz. The green variety of each is the most prized for carving.

Rhodonite, a complex silicate mineral, has an attractive pink color due to the manganese in its structure.

Rhodonite is used for carving and its hardness grading of point 6 makes it reasonably resistant to wear.

Jet

- **Jet is an organic material** that is often classified with minerals.

- **The term "jet black"** comes from this material, which is often found as layers or discrete masses in sedimentary rocks. It is therefore regarded as a sedimentary rock by many geologists.

- **Much jet** comes from the Lower Jurassic strata.

- **Jet is a type of coal**. It has a high carbon content and is formed from plant material, especially the tree *Araucaria*, commonly known as the monkey puzzle tree.

- **Unlike other types** of coal, jet is found in strata deposited in the sea. Logs and other plant remains probably drifted out into the Jurassic sea, and when waterlogged they sank, to be buried under sediment.

- **The heat and pressure** from overlying layers of sediment converted the plant material into jet.

- **Because jet** is relatively soft, it can be easily carved. It can also be very highly polished and so is used in jewelry.

▶ The modern monkey puzzle tree is a close relative of the plants from which jet formed.

▶ An ancient Roman jet bangle. Jet has been cut and worked for jewelry and ornaments for more than 2,000 years.

◀ **Jet has been cut** and polished since the Bronze Age. The ancient Romans in particular prized jewelry made from jet.

◀ **Queen Victoria** popularized jet jewelry in the 19th century after the death of her husband, Prince Albert. Jet was extensively mined at that time.

◀ **Jet has become popular** again in recent years. There are many fake items that are passed off as jet. These are usually made of man-made materials, including plastics.

Amber

- **Amber** is the fossilized resin from ancient conifer trees, and can occur in sedimentary rocks of Cenozoic Age.

- **Amber is an organic mineral** that occurs as nodules and discrete lumps.

- **As well as the typical pale orange**, it can also be brown, greenish, and black.

- **Amber is very soft** and has a splintery fracture. The surface appears resinous and transparent.

- **Much amber** is found as small "pebbles" on beaches.

- **It is only just denser** than water and can be carried by the sea. Large amounts of amber occur in the Baltic area.

- **Amber** also occurs in Romania, Italy, France, Spain, Canada, the Dominican Republic, and Russia.

◀ This fossil fly has remained unaltered since it was trapped in resin oozing from a pine tree. The resin is now amber.

▲ ◀ This necklace and two pendant stones have been made from translucent amber.

🔹 **Amber often contains** small bubbles. This is called nebulous amber.

🔹 **Amber** is very easy to carve and for many years has been used for jewelry.

🔹 **Fossils** are often found in amber. These are usually fossils of small insects that were stuck in fragrant resin oozing from a tree. This hardened to become amber.

Fossils

What are fossils?

- **Fossils** are the remains of, or evidence for, past life preserved in the rocks of the Earth's crust.

- **For the remains** of an organism to be preserved, it has to be made of material that is stable in the sediment (mud and sand) in which it is buried.

- **Usually shells**, bones, plant stems, and other remains are changed into minerals, such as calcite and quartz, for them to be preserved.

- **Creatures and plants** with hard parts are more easily preserved, as they are not easily broken before they are buried in sediment.

▲ *All living things die. Those living in water, such as this ichthyosaur, are more likely to become fossils than those on land.*

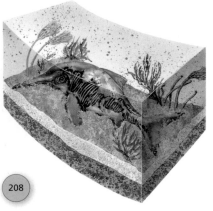

1 After death, the ichthyosaur sinks to the seabed. Worms, crabs, and other scavengers eat its soft body parts.

- **Some fossils** are simply the impressions of a shell or other organism on a rock surface. All the solid parts of the creature have disappeared.

- **Most fossils** are of organisms that lived in the sea because here most sediment is deposited.

- **Sometimes whole organisms** are preserved almost unaltered, such as insects trapped in amber or mammals preserved in frozen ground.

- **Only the tiniest fraction** of creatures and plants that have lived are preserved in the "fossil record."

- **Scientists** who study fossils are called paleontologists and the science is called paleontology.

2 Sediments cover the hard body parts, such as bones and teeth, which become fossilized.

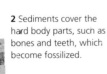

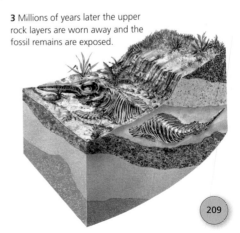

3 Millions of years later the upper rock layers are worn away and the fossil remains are exposed.

Fossils and time

- **Paleontologists** are able to use fossils to work out many details about Earth in the past, including how old strata (rock layers) are.

- **The sediments** in which fossils are preserved were deposited in layers, with the older layers below younger ones.

- **Certain strata** are characterized by particular fossils, and these rocks can be linked, or correlated, from place to place by using their fossils.

- **Fossils** that are widespread geographically are best for this linking of strata from one area to another.

- **Fossils from the Jurassic Period** found in Britain, Europe, the Himalayas, and South America tell us that rocks in these now distant regions formed at exactly the same time.

- **Fossilized species** that existed for a short time will only be found in a relatively thin layer of rock, and will allow accurate correlation.

- **Ammonites and graptolites** are excellent for the relative dating of rocks.

▼ *This large ammonite, fossilized in limestone, has been eroded to reveal the suture lines.*

- **The relative geological time scale** has been established by using fossils and other geological principles.

- **Radiometric dating** is used to give absolute dates to the various parts of the time scale.

- **The time represented** by a given fossil species is called a zone, and may be as brief as 750,000 years.

▼ *This chart shows how geological time has been divided by geologists. The absolute dates (the numbers) were worked out using radiometric dating methods.*

ERA	PERIOD	EPOCH	AGE (MYA)
CENOZOIC	Neogene	Holocene (Recent)	From 0.01
		Pleistocene	1.8–0.01
		Pliocene	5.3–1.8
		Miocene	23–5.3
	Paleogene	Oligocene	34–23
		Eocene	56–34
		Paleocene	65–55
MESOZOIC	Cretaceous		142–65
	Jurassic		206–142
	Triassic		248–206
PALEOZOIC	Permian		290–248
	Carboniferous		354–290
	Devonian		417–354
	Silurian		443–417
	Ordovician		495–443
	Cambrian		545–495
PRE-CAMBRIAN TIME			4,500–545

Extinction

◆ **When a species dies out**, for whatever reason, it is said to be extinct. Similar species may continue to survive, but that unique species has gone forever.

◆ **The fossil record** contains many breaks. A series of fossils that can be traced from layer to layer may suddenly come to an end, showing that those creatures became extinct.

◆ **Extinction** of one group of organisms can allow another to develop and flourish, so extinction allows the evolution of other species to take place.

◆ **There are countless** examples of extinction to be found when fossils are studied, from the dinosaurs to small mollusks.

◆ **The causes of extinction** are varied, but environmental changes can cause the death of many unrelated species, as may have happened at the end of the Permian Period, 248 mya.

◆ **A classic case** of extinction, which has been studied in detail, is that of the dinosaurs at the end of the Cretaceous Period, 65 mya.

◆ **There is considerable evidence** for a widespread change in climate and sea levels at the end of the Cretaceous Period.

- **Evidence** from various places shows that a large meteorite may have hit Earth at about this time.

- **Dust from this meteorite impact** would obscure the sunlight and kill plants. Food chains would then be destroyed, causing widespread extinction of many different animals.

DID YOU KNOW?

When the dinosaurs became extinct, so did 75 percent of marine plankton, and very successful creatures such as the marine ammonites.

◀▶ Ammonite fossils. Ammonites became extinct at the end of the Cretaceous Period, 65 mya.

213

Evolution

🐚 **Evidence** for the development of life into its various forms can be found in the record of fossils. This change from one living thing to another is called evolution.

🐚 **By looking at fossils**, it can clearly be seen that the more primitive plants and animals are found in the oldest rocks. However, the trilobites, which occurred as long ago as the Cambrian Period (545–495 mya), were very well-developed creatures.

🐚 **Evolution** is not always a steady process. It has many sudden jumps when organisms develop rapidly.

▼ ▶ *Many different kinds of trilobites evolved and died out over millions of years.*

🐚 **During the Pre-Cambrian Era** (before 545 mya) life was probably very primitive, but for various reasons the fossil record from this time is extremely sparse.

Angelina
490 mya

🐚 **At the start** of the Cambrian Period, a rapid explosion of life-forms occurred. Trilobites and many other invertebrates were suddenly numerous.

🐚 **In the Jurassic Period** (206–142 mya) sea urchins suddenly developed and evolved.

Charles Darwin's famous book on evolution *The Origin of the Species* was published in 1859. His theories of natural selection and the survival of the organisms best suited to a certain habitat are still accepted by most scientists today.

Trinucleus
450 mya

Modern scientists are trying to increase our knowledge of evolution. Darwin didn't have access to new scientific ideas about DNA and genetics.

Mutation is one of the keys to evolution. It is a change in the DNA of an organism, which may occur because of chemical or environmental influence.

Kolihapeltis
400 mya

Humans have influenced the evolution of various organisms. Where industrial pollution has produced dark, grimy tree trunks, a dark form of the peppered moth has evolved, which is camouflaged in this habitat. Human misuse of the environment has driven many species to extinction.

Tracks, trails, and burrows

◀ **Sedimentary rocks** can be formed as layers on the seabed, the land surface, a lake, or river bed. These layers (strata) were at one time the Earth's surface, and they often have puzzling grooves and trails running over them.

◀ **Along with a wide range** of other structures, these trails are called trace fossils.

◀ **A fossil**, the record of past life, does not have to be a shell, bone, or leaf. It can be a burrow, track, eggshell, or dropping that tells us that a creature or plant has existed.

◀ **The study** of these trace fossils is called ichnology.

◀ **Trace fossils** are given scientific names, like other fossils.

◀ **Some of the most famous** trace fossils are dinosaur footprints. These can be used to work out the size and speed of a dinosaur.

▲ These grooves were probably made by mollusks moving over wet mud on the Carboniferous seabed.

🔹 **For a trace fossil**, such as a burrow or arthropod track, to be preserved, it must be filled in with mud or sand very soon after it is made, or it will be washed away.

🔹 **In some cases**, the fossil of the mollusk or shrimp that has made a trace fossil is found at the end of its fossil burrow.

🔹 **Dinosaur eggs** are trace fossils. Nests of *Protoceratops'* eggs and young have been found in Mongolia, Asia.

🔹 **A trace fossil** called *Cruziana* occurs in many strata of Paleozoic and Mesozoic age. Originally, it was thought to be the trail of a trilobite, but these arthropods became extinct in the late Paleozoic. It is possible that a number of different arthropods made very similar trails.

▼ *Footprints left in wet mud may become fossilized. The size and speed of the animal that made them can often be calculated.*

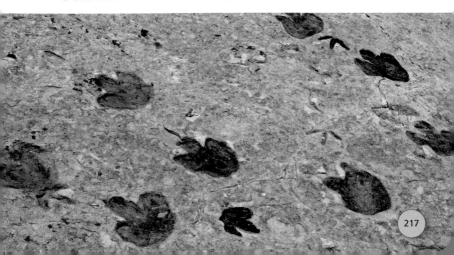

Microfossils

 Microfossils are tiny fossils that can only be studied with the help of a microscope. There is no actual agreed size below which a fossil is considered to be a microfossil. When seen at high magnification, microfossils reveal a remarkable array of shapes and structures.

 The larger fossils, such as shells, bones, teeth, and plant remains, are called macrofossils.

 Microfossils are widespread and commonly overlooked. Most sedimentary rocks contain microfossils, and a study of these can give important details about the age and environment in which the rock was formed.

 Many microfossils are of single-celled organisms, and the use of an electron microscope is necessary to study them.

 The study of fossil pollen, palynology, is a branch of micropaleontology. Pollen is a very good indicator of past climates.

DID YOU KNOW?
The pure white limestone called chalk is made up of microfossils including coccoliths. These are single-celled, planktonic organisms with a circular structure. They are most numerous in warm seawater.

 At certain points in the geological record there are rocks referred to as cherts. These are silica-rich sediments, some of which are formed by accumulations of microfossils called *Radiolaria*.

▲ *Among the most common fossils are minute microfossils. These diatoms (minute, single-celled algae) are magnified many hundreds of times.*

Conodonts are minute, toothlike fossils. Exactly what they are has been a matter of discussion. Studies of complete conodont fossils suggest that it may have been an creature similar to an eel. They only occur in rocks from the Cambrian to Triassic ages.

Foraminifera are single-celled organisms that live as plankton or on the seabed. Their tiny shells make up much of the "ooze" that covers the deep ocean floor.

Nummulites are slightly larger types of Foraminifera that often make up nummulitic limestone. This rock was used a lot as a building stone in ancient Egypt.

219

The oldest fossils

The record of fossils from Precambrian times (4,600–545 mya) is remarkably sparse. This is most of geological time, and yet we know very little about what was alive then.

Precambrian rocks are often changed by metamorphism, and so any fossils they may have contained could have been removed.

Primitive life-forms would have had soft bodies, probably without shells, so may not have been preserved as fossils.

In its early years, Earth's atmosphere lacked oxygen and may have been composed of gases such as water vapor, methane, and ammonia. These are not useful to life as we know it today.

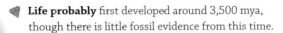

🔹 **Life probably** first developed around 3,500 mya, though there is little fossil evidence from this time.

🔹 **Among the earliest** fossils are 3,500 million-year-old algal remains found in Western Australia.

🔹 **In the silica-rich** chert near Lake Superior in the U.S., fossil microscopic plant cells occur, suggesting that there was more oxygen about.

🔹 **Late in the Precambrian Period**, organisms became more numerous. One of the most famous groups of fossils, the "Ediacaran assemblage," comes from a number of sites, including Australia, England, Newfoundland, Scandinavia, Russia, and Africa.

🔹 **Ediacaran fossils** include delicate organisms such as jellyfish, worms, frondlike organisms, and sea pens.

🔹 *Charnia* is a famous Ediacaran fossil found in 1957 in Charnwood Forest, Leicestershire, U.K., by a schoolboy.

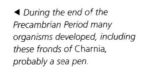

◄ During the end of the Precambrian Period many organisms developed, including these fronds of Charnia, probably a sea pen.

221

Fossil algae

- **Though they are very delicate organisms**, certain algae build calcium carbonate structures that are easily preserved as fossils.

- **The best-known fossil** algal structures are called stromatolites, made by blue-green algae.

- **Algae and bacteria** work together to build the rounded mounds of layered calcium carbonate.

- **When seen in a rock face**, stromatolites are mounds of calcite. On a flat surface they look like concentrically banded disks.

- **The earliest stromatolites** are found in rocks more than 3,000 million years old.

- **In the 1950s**, living stromatolite-building algae were found in Western Australia. Here they exist in water that is highly saline, where other organisms can't survive.

- **Much Precambrian** limestone is the result of stromatolite formation.

- **Blue-green algae** produce oxygen. This vital gas began to accumulate in Earth's early atmosphere, allowing evolution to develop oxygen-dependent organisms.

- **This abundance of oxygen** led to the formation of the ozone layer high in the atmosphere, which protects us from harmful ultraviolet radiation.

- **Stromatolites** have occurred on Earth for thousands of millions of years.

▼ Found in shallow sea water, these living stromatolites in Western Australia are almost identical to those that first evolved in Precambrian time, 3,000 million years ago.

Primitive plants

🔸 **The first vascular plants** (plants with veins) evolved in the late Paleozoic Era.

🔸 **In Devonian rocks** there is evidence of a rapid evolution of plants, and the Earth's surface began to look green for the first time.

🔸 *Cooksonia* is a very early veined plant and occurred in rocks of late Silurian and Devonian age. During this period there were large landmasses on which vegetation could develop.

🔸 **Like modern plants**, *Cooksonia* had xylem cells that were able to transport water through the plant.

🔸 **The fossil plant *Parka*** is also from the Devonian Period. Both *Cooksonia* and *Parka* probably reproduced with spores.

◀ *This reconstruction of* Cooksonia *shows its delicate branching stems and fruiting masses.*

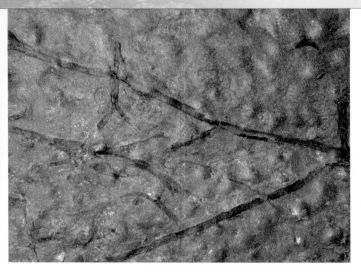

▲ *These slender stems of* Cooksonia, *one of the first land plants, were found in rocks of Devonian age in Orkney, Scotland.*

🔹 **Like many fossil plants**, these early Devonian species are preserved as thin carbon films, the rest of the plant tissue being lost during fossilization.

🔹 **One of the best** examples of early plant preservation is a rock formation called the Rhynie chert, found in Devonian rocks in Scotland. Here, early plants are preserved three-dimensionally in silica.

🔹 **Microscope analysis** of these silica fossils shows all their soft parts, allowing cellular structures to be examined.

🔹 **It is probable that the Rhynie chert** was deposited by hot springs, the plant remains washing in from nearby.

Coal-forming plants

▼ These alternating coal, shale, and sandstone strata are on the coast of Fife, Scotland. The darker layers are coal, made from plants that grew in the Carboniferous delta forests.

- **The richest deposits of coal** have been formed by the accumulation of peat from forests. Coal-forming forests flourished in the Carboniferous Period.

- **As these forests grew** on the swampy top of vast deltas, they were flooded by the sea many times. This flooding brought sand and silt onto the deltas, in which fossil plants are often preserved.

- **A great variety of plants** grew in Carboniferous forests, including giant horsetails, clubmosses, and seed ferns.

- *Lepidodendron* is a common fossil clubmoss from Carboniferous strata. It grew to more than 100 ft in height. The roots of this clubmoss are usually found as separate fossils, called *Stigmaria*.

- *Lepidodendron* **stems** can be recognized by their diamond-shaped leaf scars.

- **Another common** Carboniferous coal fossil is the giant horsetail, *Calamites*. Today, horsetails are relatively small plants that live in damp ground. *Calamites* grew to around 100 ft tall.

- **Horsetails** have soft tissue inside their stems, which decays rapidly when they die. During fossilization, the stems often filled with sediment, so they are preserved in three dimensions.

- **A group of smaller plants** that helped make coal were called seed ferns.

- **Seed ferns** are plants with fernlike leaves, often preserved as carbon films on bedding planes.

- **Common Carboniferous** seed ferns include *Neuropteris*, *Eupecopteris*, and *Sphenopteris*.

Mazon Creek, Illinois

◀ **At certain times** in the fossil record a number of remarkably detailed accumulations of fossils occurred.

◀ **At Mazon Creek in Illinois**, U.S., coal has been strip-mined for many tens of years. Above the coal layers there are mudstones, in which rounded, iron-rich lumps, called nodules, occur.

◀ **Nodules like these** are common in mudstone and shale of different ages. Their importance is that fossils contained in them are often beautifully preserved in great detail.

◀ **It is thought** that these, and nodules in other strata, often form chemically around organic remains.

◀ **Plant fossils**, especially leaves, are commonly crushed on bedding planes, but in the Mazon Creek nodules, leaves are three-dimensional.

◀ **As well as perfect plants**, these rocks contain an amazing variety of other fossils, and geologists can work out the details of the habitats in which they lived.

◀ *The delicate leaflets of the seed fern* Neuropteris *have been preserved as a carbon film inside an ironstone nodule.*

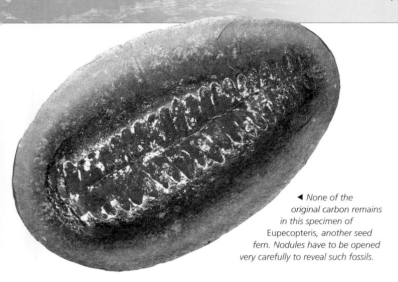

◀ None of the original carbon remains in this specimen of Eupecopteris, another seed fern. Nodules have to be opened very carefully to reveal such fossils.

🔹 **Marine and freshwater** creatures are found here. Fossils of jellyfish (only preserved in ideal circumstances), worms, amphibians, and fish all occur in the Mazon Creek strata.

🔹 **As often occurs in cases of exceptional fossilization**, there are fossils of soft-bodied creatures that are otherwise unknown.

🔹 **Other examples** of nodules containing exceptional fossils are those from the Carboniferous rocks of Lancashire, U.K., and the ammonite-bearing nodules of the British Lower Jurassic.

> DID YOU KNOW?
>
> Spiders, scorpions, centipedes, and millipedes are fossilized at Mazon Creek, giving us a glimpse into a Carboniferous world that is unknown elsewhere.

Glossopteris and continental drift

🔹 *Glossopteris* is an extinct seed fern. Its fossils occur in the southern landmasses of Antarctica, Australia, New Zealand, South America, and southern Africa.

🔹 **This plant** had a treelike appearance and was up to 20 ft tall.

🔹 **Usually only** the delicately veined leaves are found as fossils.

🔹 **One of the most famous** geological books is *The Origins of Continents and Oceans*, written by Alfred Wegener, and published in 1924.

🔹 **In this book**, Wegener puts together evidence to prove that the southern continents were at one time joined as a single landmass and have now drifted apart to their present positions.

🔹 **Wegener was not a geologist** but a meteorologist, and his ideas were initially dismissed by the leading geologists of the time.

🔹 **Because *Glossopteris*** occurs in the southern continents, which are now hundreds of miles away from each other, Wegener was able to use it as one of his key pieces of evidence to show that these areas had once been joined.

🔹 **The problem** when he put forward his theory was that no one understood how the continents could move.

▶ Glossopteris *grew to around 20 ft in height. It may have grown with a treelike or bushy habit.*

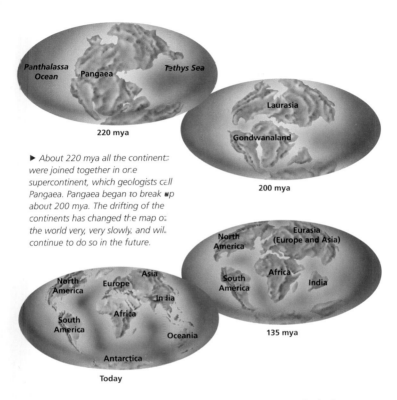

220 mya

200 mya

135 mya

Today

▶ About 220 mya all the continents were joined together in one supercontinent, which geologists call Pangaea. Pangaea began to break up about 200 mya. The drifting of the continents has changed the map of the world very, very slowly, and will continue to do so in the future.

◀ **Today we have the knowledge** of plate tectonics, which shows how the ocean basins form and how the continents move, proving that Wegener was correct.

◀ **The theory of plate tectonics** shows that the continents move at about 0.9 in a year—this is the same speed at which your fingernails grow.

Ginkgo and other living fossils

🔹 **The expression "living fossil"** is often used to describe a plant or animal that occurs as a fossil in rocks formed many millions of years ago, and also lives today.

🔹 **Living fossils** have been changed very little by evolution and have a very stable habitat and way of life.

🔹 *Ginkgo biloba*, the maidenhair tree, is grown in many countries as an ornamental tree, and is prized for its medicinal properties.

🔹 **In China**, *Ginkgo* was cultivated in temple gardens as a sacred tree. It was thought to be extinct until some were found in the wild in southeast China in 1956.

▼ *Fossil leaves of Ginkgo from Jurassic strata in North Yorkshire, U.K.*

▶ A leaf from the modern maidenhair tree, Ginkgo biloba, is very similar to the Jurassic fossil leaves.

- **Leaves of *Ginkgo*,** usually preserved as carbon impressions, have been fossilized in rocks from the Permian Period (290–248 mya).

- **Fossilized *Ginkgo*** leaves are virtually the same as those of the living tree.

- **The leaves of *Ginkgo*** are very distinctive, being almost triangular in shape and partly indented.

- **Some of the best** *Ginkgo* fossils are from Jurassic strata on the coast of North Yorkshire, U.K.,

- **The brachiopod shellfish,** *Lingula,* occurs in rocks of Cambrian age (545–495 mya). It is one of the earliest examples of a living fossil.

DID YOU KNOW?

Other well-known living fossils include the coelacanth, a fish thought to have been extinct for more than 60 million years until one was caught off the coast of South Africa in 1938.

Mesozoic and Cenozoic plants

🔹 **Many ferns and fernlike plants** are fossilized in rocks formed during the Jurassic Period.

🔹 *Coniopteris* is a fern found in Jurassic rocks. It occurs in North America, Europe, and Asia.

🔹 **Another common Jurassic plant** is *Williamsonia*. This is an extinct plant with fernlike leaves, which are usually preserved as black carbon films on bedding surfaces. It had cones rather than typical modern flowers.

▼ *These delicate leaves are from the fernlike Jurassic plant,* Williamsonia, *which flourished in the swamp forests of the middle Jurassic Period.*

▶ A fossil cone of the extinct plant Williamsonia.

🔹 **The evolution** of flowering plants began toward the middle of the Mesozoic Era.

🔹 **There is evidence** that plants with flowerlike structures lived early in the Cretaceous Period (142–65 mya), but fossils of true flowers only occur toward the late Cretaceous.

🔹 **Much of the evidence** that early plants bore flowers comes from fossil pollen.

🔹 **Fossil pollen** is invaluable in helping to work out changes in the climate of the past.

DID YOU KNOW?

Flowers provide a way for plants to evolve, as pollen can combine the genes of one plant with those of another.

🔹 **The evolution of insects** is closely linked to the development of flowering plants. Insects feed on nectar and pollen, and carry pollen from flower to flower.

🔹 **Fossil insects** are often perfectly preserved in amber, the hardened resin from pine and similar trees.

235

Fossil corals

🔹 **Much limestone**, especially that deposited during the Paleozoic Era, consists of fossilized corals and coral fragments.

🔹 **The earliest corals** are simple "tabulate" corals, which first appeared as fossils in rocks of the Ordovician Period.

🔹 **Tabulate corals** have a tubular structure and may be attached to others to form a colony. The tube (corallite) is divided horizontally by sheets of calcite called tabulae.

🔹 **The coral organism**, or polyp, was rather like a small sea anemone, and lived at the top of the tube.

🔹 **Tabulate corals** became extinct in the Permian Period.

🔹 ***Dibunophyllum*** belongs to a group called the "rugose" corals. These are more complex than the tabulate group.

In the Silurian and Carboniferous Periods, rugose corals built large, shallow sea reefs, in which numerous fossils of corals, brachiopods, mollusks, crinoids, and trilobites have been found.

The rugose corals became extinct at a similar time to the tabulate corals, in the Permian Period.

Some corals in the Carboniferous Period are used as zone fossils. Each coral species represents a small part of geological time.

Modern corals began to evolve early in the Mesozoic Era.

◀ *The delicate internal structure of corals is often well preserved in fossils, as seen in this species,* Dibunophyllum.

Jurassic reefs

- **The corals that evolved** during the Mesozoic Era, in the shallow sea reefs of the Jurassic Period, were different from those of the Paleozoic Era.

- **Jurassic corals** are classified as Scleractinian corals. They are also called hexacorals because they have six internal divisions.

- **Scleractinian corals** have many similarities to corals that live in tropical seas today.

- *Isastrea* **is a typical Jurassic coral** that flourished in warm, clear seawater with little mud suspended in it.

- **Modern tropical corals** require similar conditions, of warm, clear water through which sunlight can penetrate.

- *Isastrea* grew as a mass of small, joined, individual corallites standing upright on the seabed.

- **When a lot of muddy sediment** was deposited, the coral reefs died out.

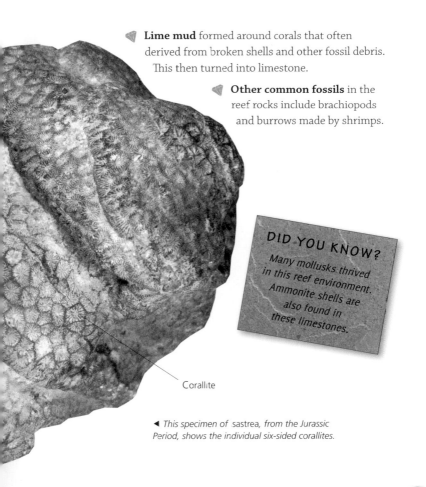

Lime mud formed around corals that often derived from broken shells and other fossil debris. This then turned into limestone.

Other common fossils in the reef rocks include brachiopods and burrows made by shrimps.

DID YOU KNOW?
Many mollusks thrived in this reef environment. Ammonite shells are also found in these limestones.

Corallite

◄ This specimen of sastrea, from the Jurassic Period, shows the individual six-sided corallites.

Fossil sponges

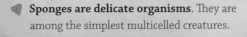

🔸 **Sponges are mostly marine animals** that live in various habitats, and can be found today in low-shore rock pools.

🔸 **Sponges are delicate organisms**. They are among the simplest multicelled creatures.

▶ *This modern tropical vase sponge has a feather star growing on it. Feather stars are closely related to starfish and sea urchins.*

▶ Raphidonema *is a fossil vase sponge common during the Mesozoic Era.*

🔹 **A sponge** is made of a thin, porous structure, which is supported by small spines called spicules. Spicules are sometimes made of silica, a resistant material that may make up certain rock materials such as chert.

🔹 **Surprisingly**, despite their structure, sponges are not uncommon as fossils.

🔹 **Rocks** as old as the Cambrian Period contain fossil sponges.

🔹 *Raphidonema* is a well-known fossil sponge found in Mesozoic rocks.

🔹 **Some fossil sponges**, including *Siphonia,* have long stems and stand on the seabed. They look like tulips.

🔹 *Raphidonema* has a structure like a porous, crinkled vase. It grew from the seabed, with its wide opening pointing upwards.

🔹 **Sponges form** part of a community of marine creatures. Often there are fossils of bivalve mollusks such as oysters and pectens, and also gastropods and ammonites found with the fossil sponges.

Fossil crinoids

◀ **Crinoids are strange animals**, which have a plantlike structure. They have roots, a stem, and a cup (calyx) at the top, in which the animal lives.

◀ **Because of their structure**, crinoids are also called "sea lilies."

◀ **The solid parts** of the structure are made of calcite, which means crinoids are easily fossilized. However, it is usually only the stem that is preserved.

◀ **The stem is composed** of numerous small disks called ossicles. Before and during fossilization, the stem of a crinoid often breaks. Some crinoidal limestone is composed almost entirely of ossicles.

◀ **Above the calyx** are flexible, feathery arms. These direct water currents containing food toward the animal.

◀ **Crinoids** are closely related to starfish and sea urchins. All three groups of creatures belong to the phylum Echinodermata.

◀ **Traumatocrinus**, from the Triassic rocks of the Ghizou Province, China, shows the flexible stems and calyx with waving arms.

◀ **Crinoids** first evolved during the Ordovician Period.

◀ **Not all crinoids live** attached by their roots to the seabed. Some are free-swimming.

◀ **Today**, crinoids live in all depths of seawater. Some are even found in the deepest abyssal water.

▶ *Each of these specimens of* Traumatocrinus *has a calyx, stem, and arms.*

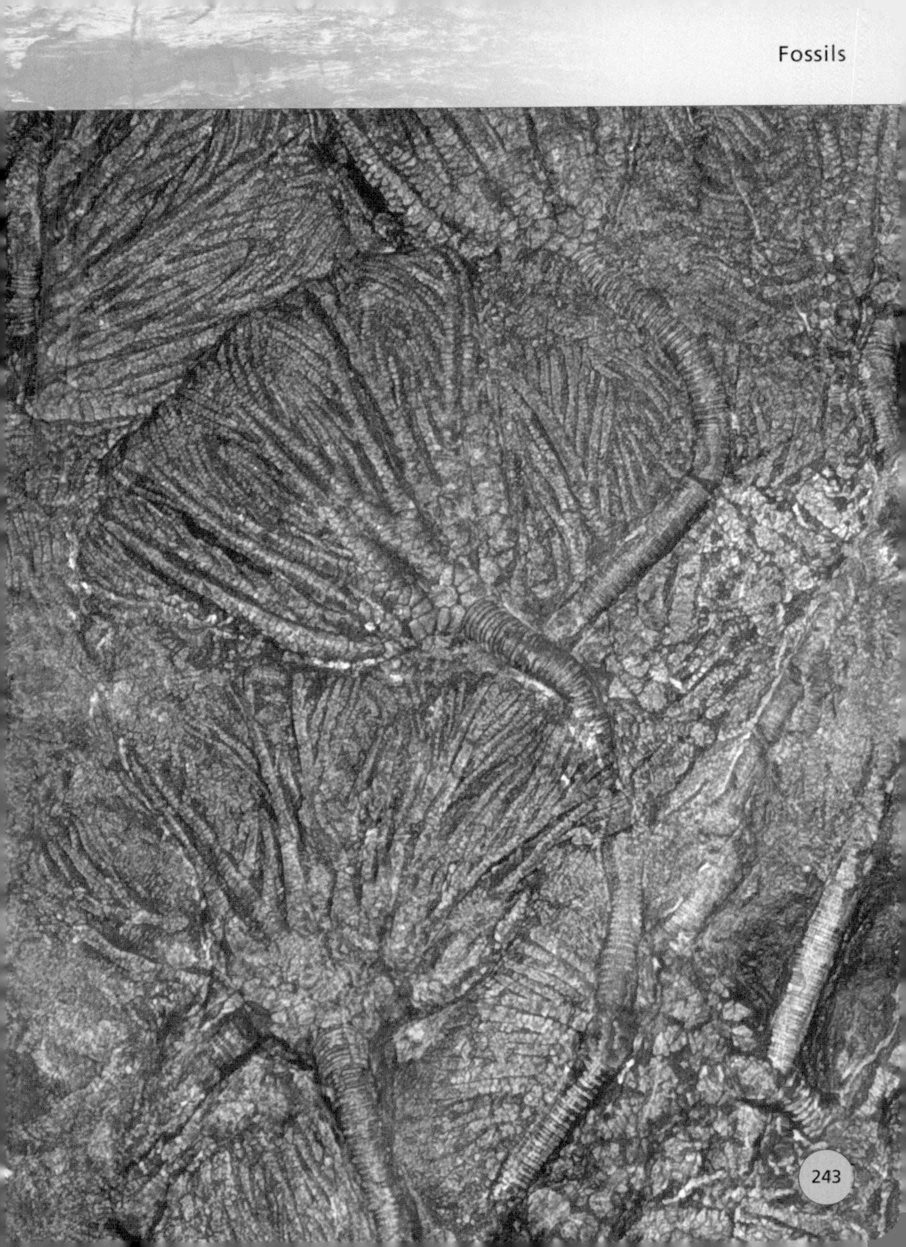

Brittle stars

- **Brittle stars** are delicate starfish with long, slender arms. Usually there are five arms, giving them typical echinoderm symmetry.

- **As in other starfish**, the animal's mouth is in the central disk. The flexible arms allow the creature to move rapidly over the seabed.

- **Many brittle stars** feed on plankton, but some species eat small shellfish.

- **Fossils** of brittle stars, which are scientifically called ophiuroids, are found in rocks dating as far back as the Ordovician Period.

- **There are a number** of "starfish beds" in the fossil record, some of the best being found in lower Jurassic rocks.

- **Other numbers** of brittle stars have been found in Devonian rocks in Germany and Silurian strata in Scotland, U.K.

- **Today**, brittle stars often live in large numbers in both shallow and deep seas.

- **Because brittle stars are so delicate**, the possibility of them being washed together by sea currents and fossilized as a large number of perfect specimens is remote.

- **For a mass of brittle stars** to be fossilized together, it is likely that a colony was rapidly covered with mud or sand.

- **It has been discovered** that living brittle stars cannot escape from sediment more than 2 in deep.

◄ *This fossil mass of brittle stars shows the central disk and flexible arms, all with five-fold symmetry.*

Spiny sea urchins

- **Sea urchins** use their spines for moving about and as protection from predators.

- **The spines** on sea urchins vary greatly. Some echinoids have a few stout, club-shaped spines and others have a mass of slender, pointed spines.

- *Cidaris* is a fossil sea urchin from rocks of Jurassic to Recent age.

- **On its shell**, *Cidaris* has large, rounded "bosses" where the spines were attached with a ball-and-socket joint.

- **Often the shell breaks** up during fossilization, and the large spines are frequently found as individual fossils.

- *Cidaris* **has a rounded shell** with the mouth central below, and is classified as a regular echinoid.

- **In rocks of Jurassic age**, *Cidaris* is found in limestone strata with many other fossils. These include corals, brachiopods, mollusks, and bryozoans.

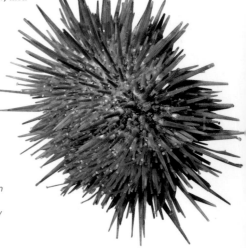

▶ Psammechinus, *also known as the green sea urchin, is a modern sea urchin with many thin, sharp spines.*

▲ *Delicate echinoid spines are rarely preserved as fossils. The Jurassic sea urchin* Cidaris *is very similar to the modern-day* Psammechinus.

🔹 ***Psammechinus*** is a spiny sea urchin that lives today in shallow seas, and can be found in rock pools on the shore at low tide.

🔹 **The spines** on *Psammechinus* are relatively large. They are attached to the outside of the shell in a similar way to those on the fossil *Cidaris.*

🔹 **As with fossil sea urchins**, the spines break off *Psammechinus* when it dies. Empty shells washed up on the shore rarely have spines attached to them.

Burrowing sea urchins

- **Sea urchins** that burrow into the soft sediment on the seabed are often heart-shaped in outline.

- *Micraster* is a common fossil sea urchin. It is found in chalk formed in the Cretaceous Period.

- **Because of its unusual outline**, *Micraster* is classified as an irregular echinoid.

- **Other features** that make it irregular are its very short, petal-shaped rows of plates, and the non-central position of the mouth and anus.

- *Micraster* has been the subject of many scientific studies. An evolutionary sequence of this genus has been worked out.

- **The chalk** in which fossils of *Micraster* are found was formed as a fine mud on the seabed.

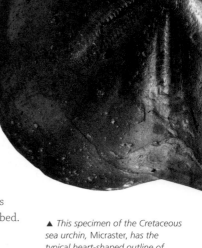

▲ This specimen of the Cretaceous sea urchin, Micraster, has the typical heart-shaped outline of a burrowing echinoid.

🔺 **Other fossils** found with *Micraster* include bivalve mollusks, sponges, corals, brachiopods, and fish teeth.

🔺 ***Echinocardium* is a modern** sea urchin that lives in shallow seas. It burrows into mud and sand.

🔺 **This recent sea urchin** has a heart-shaped shell, very similar to that of *Micraster*.

🔺 **Though *Echinocardium* is covered** with soft spines when alive, dead shells washed up on the shore are usually bare of spines.

▼ *Echinocardium is a common echinoid around the coast of Britain. Its scientific name means "spiny heart." It is a burrower, like the fossil* Micraster.

249

Brachiopods

Brachiopods are marine shellfish that are very different from other shelled animals. They are classified in a phylum of their own and are commonly known as lampshells.

A typical brachiopod has a shell made of two valves. Some brachiopods are able to open and close their shells to let in seawater containing food.

The two valves of a brachiopod shell differ from each other. One valve has a hole in its pointed end through which a tough stalk sticks out. This stalk, called the pedicle, anchors the animal to the seabed.

Inarticulate brachiopods are the most primitive, and were first found fossilized in Ordovician strata.

▼ *Brachiopods are marine shellfish, which were numerous in the past. These fossil brachiopods are from Silurian strata in Norway.*

- *Lingula* is an inarticulate brachiopod, as it can't open and close its shell.

- **This brachiopod** burrows vertically into soft mud on the seabed.

DID YOU KNOW?

Lingula is called a living fossil because it has remained virtually unchanged for 500 million years.

- **Modern-day *Lingula*** can help paleontologists suggest what habitat this brachiopod lived in before they became fossilized.

- **Primitive brachiopods**, such as *Lingula*, have different shell compositions from other brachiopods. *Lingula's* shell is made of phosphates and chitin—a similar material to human fingernails.

  - *Lingula* is found fossilized in dark shales and mudstones with other brachiopods and bivalve mollusks.

Paleozoic brachiopods

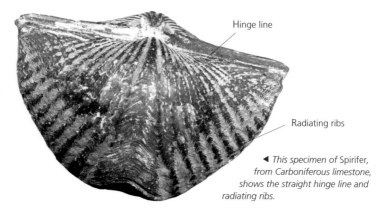

Hinge line

Radiating ribs

◄ *This specimen of* Spirifer, *from Carboniferous limestone, shows the straight hinge line and radiating ribs.*

- **Brachiopods** still live today, but they were far more numerous in the past than they are now.

- **During the Carboniferous Period**, many brachiopods, including *Spirifer* and *Productus*, lived in the shallow seas that covered much of Europe and North America.

- ***Spirifer* and *Productus*** are called articulate brachiopods because they could open and close their shells.

- **The symmetry** of a brachiopod shell is different from that of a bivalve mollusk. A bivalve has two valves that are similar to each other. A brachiopod's two valves differ from each other.

- ***Spirifer*** has a small shell crossed with thick ridges called ribs. There is a straight hinge line along which the shell opens.

- *Productus* is a different shape from *Spirifer*. It is more rounded, and some species grew quite large. *Gigantoproductus* commonly grew to 6 in across.

- **The shell** of *Productus* is covered with circular growth lines and thin radiating ribs.

- *Productus* often has a spiny shell, though the delicate spines break off easily during fossilization. These spines may have helped to anchor the shell in mud on the seabed.

- **Both of these brachiopods** are commonly found in limestone of the Carboniferous Period.

- **Other fossils** found with *Productus* and *Spirifer* include corals, trilobites, and mollusks.

▶ Productus is a common fossil brachiopod. A few of the spines used to anchor the shell into the mud of the seabed can be seen here.

Spines

Rhynchonellids

🐚 **Small brachiopods** with heavily ribbed shells are common in many Jurassic strata. These are classified as Rhynchonellids.

🐚 **The shell** of a typical Rhynchonellid has a diameter of only 2 in.

🐚 **They are articulate brachiopods**, which could open and close their shells. The larger pedicle valve has a hole from which the fleshy pedicle protruded.

🐚 **The shell** is made of calcite, unlike the phosphatic shell of the inarticulate brachiopods.

🐚 **This group** seems to have been very successful, and first evolved during the Ordovician Period. Some species still live today.

🐚 **A notable feature** of the shell is the zigzag line along which the shell opens.

🐚 **These brachiopods** are found in a number of different Jurassic strata. They are most common in limestones and ironstones, and also occur in sandstones.

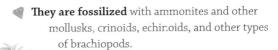

They are fossilized with ammonites and other mollusks, crinoids, echinoids, and other types of brachiopods.

Rhynchonellids are often fossilized in small clusters. It is probable that they lived attached in groups to the seabed.

From the strata in which they are fossilized, it can be worked out that these brachiopods preferred clear seawater, without much sand or mud.

1	Thecosmilia
2	Bryozoan
3	Chlamys
4	Rhynchonellids
5	Cladophyllia conybeari
6	Trochid
7	Rhabdophyllia

▲ *Small Rhynchonellid brachiopods lived attached to the seabed. In this reef habitat, numerous other organisms were common, including corals, mollusks, and echinoids.*

255

Graptolites

- **Graptolites** were simple marine animals that first appeared in the Cambrian Period. They then became extinct in the Carboniferous Period.

- **Graptolite** fossils are found in rocks that formed in the deep sea, such as dark mudstones and shales. The name "graptolite" means "writing in stone."

- **A typical graptolite**, such as *Didymograptus,* has a slender, elongated structure, often only one to 2 in long. This is called the stipe.

- **When examined in detail**, a graptolite's stipe has a series of small projections on one or both sides, giving the appearance of the teeth found on a saw. These are called thecae, and in life were small cups in which tiny marine creatures called zooids lived.

▼ *Many different types of graptolite evolved. Some had single stipes, such as* Monograptus. *Others, such as* Dictyonema, *joined together in a colony.*

- **The graptolite** is the structure built up by a colony of zooids and was either anchored to the seabed, or in other cases, floated on ocean currents.

Orthograptus

Dictyonema

- **Originally, graptolites** were classified with small colonial marine organisms called hydrozoans. In the 1940s, their classification was reorganized, when their biology was closely examined.

- **Graptolites are classified** in their own phylum, the Hemichordata, which also includes acorn worms and pterobranchs.

- **Because they are so delicate**, graptolites are preserved in only the finest-grained sedimentary rocks. They often occur in great masses, looking like pencil marks on the bedding planes.

- **Sometimes** they are preserved in iron pyrite, and three-dimensional preservation occurs in rare cases.

- **Graptolites evolved** into many different species, and in some rocks are very common fossils.

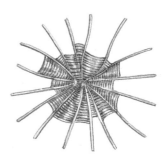

Monograptus   *Phyllograptus*   *Loganograptus*

Arthropods

◀ **Arthropods** are one of the most varied and successful groups of creatures to have evolved.

◀ **The first arthropods** are found fossilized in rocks of Cambrian age. They are still numerous in all manner of habitats today.

◀ **The scientific name** for the arthropod group is phylum Arthropoda. It contains creatures that can fly, swim, burrow, and sting.

◀ **Butterflies and moths**, crabs and lobsters, shrimps, centipedes, spiders, and scorpions are all arthropods.

◀ **These creatures** have a tough outer skin (exoskeleton), which protects and holds together the soft body.

◀ **As an arthropod grows**, it sheds its exoskeleton. Many pass through a larval stage, and molt as the larva grows.

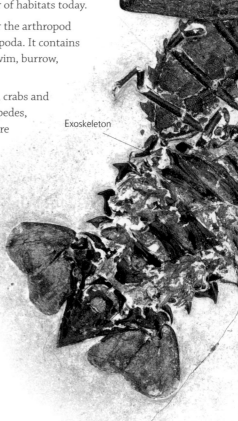

Exoskeleton

Feeler

Claw

Leg

◀ *Eryon is an arthropod from Jurassic strata. It was an early member of the crab and lobster group, Decapoda. The segmented exoskeleton, legs, feelers, and claws have been perfectly preserved.*

Some arthropods have claws, others have wings and most have segmented legs and thin, flexible feelers.

Perhaps the best-known fossil arthropods are trilobites. Many trilobite fossils may be the remains of shed exoskeletons.

Eryon is a marine arthropod that probably lived on the seabed.

Many arthropods have excellent vision. Trilobites were the first known animals with complex eyes that could form detailed images.

Fossil insects

Insects have all the main features of the arthropods. Many of them are also able to fly.

Even though they are delicate, insects have a tough exoskeleton. For this reason, the fossil record of insects is surprisingly good.

Insects often need special circumstances to become fossilized. Very fine-grained, dustlike sediment helps to preserve delicate details.

Many insects have been preserved in amber, the hardened resin that oozes from pine and similar trees. Insects that got stuck in the resin could become perfectly fossilized.

◄ *This delicate fossilized mayfly is from rocks of Cretaceous age in Brazil. Even the wings have been preserved in the very fine-grained sediment.*

▶ This 100–million–year–old dragonfly is one of thousands from Brazil's Santana Formation rocks.

🔸 **Because many insects** live on land, their fossils are less common than sea-dwelling arthropods.

🔸 **Insects** first appeared as fossils in rocks of Devonian age.

🔸 **During the Carboniferous Period**, giant dragonflies flew over the swamps that covered much of Europe and North America.

🔸 **Some insects** pass through various stages of development (metamorphosis). Fossils of caterpillars and chrysalids have been found in rocks of Mesozoic age.

🔸 **The first insects** were probably predators. When flowering plants developed in the Mesozoic Era, they provided pollen and nectar as food for many insects. In turn, insects carried pollen from flower to flower, and helped to fertilize plants.

🔸 **It has been suggested** that insect DNA could be recovered from fossils in amber. This is highly unlikely, as the chemical structure of DNA breaks down quickly.

Giant trilobites

- **Trilobites** are probably the best-known group of fossil arthropods. They are first found in rocks from the Cambrian Period.

- **Along with many different creatures**, trilobites became extinct during the Permian Period.

- **Trilobites** were advanced marine creatures, with a complex, three-lobed structure. They had a central axis and two lateral lobes, hence the name trilobite, which means three lobes.

- **They had a head shield** (cephalon), which in many types, including *Paradoxides*, had eyes. The central nervous system was probably here. *Paradoxides* had long spines extending back from the edges of the head shield.

- **The exoskeleton** was flexible, and *Paradoxides* was able to move across the seabed, using legs attached underneath.

- *Paradoxides* was a much larger trilobite. Its fossilized remains occur in Cambrian rocks in Europe, North and South America, and north Africa. It is used as a zone fossil to date rocks relatively.

DID YOU KNOW?

Most trilobites were about 2 in or less in length. Paradoxides grew much larger. Some giants were up to 24 in long.

- **It is a puzzle** to paleontologists why creatures as complex and advanced as trilobites have no apparent ancestors. They are present in the Cambrian strata, but not before that.

🔹 **Precambrian rocks** are often metamorphosed and altered, so any fossils in them would have been destroyed. However, there are marine sedimentary strata of late Precambrian times without any trace of trilobites in them.

🔹 **Their ancestors** may have been soft-bodied creatures, which could not have become fossilized. Trilobites probably developed exoskeletons early in the Cambrian Period, and then would have been readily fossilized.

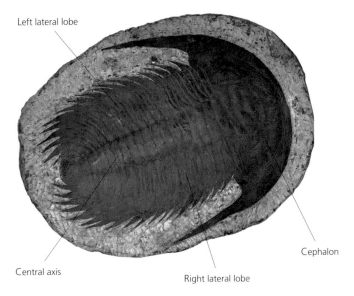

Left lateral lobe

Cephalon

Central axis

Right lateral lobe

▲ *This specimen of* Paradoxides *comes from early Cambrian strata in Morocco.*

Ogyginus and Trinucleus

🔹 **These two trilobites** occur in rocks of Ordovician age. They are well-known from strata of this age in Britain, and also occur elsewhere in Europe.

🔹 *Ogyginus* **is a medium-sized trilobite**. Specimens are typically up to 2 in long. However, some are more than 4 in long.

🔹 **This trilobite** is obviously in three parts, with a definite central lobe extending from the thorax to the head shield and tail section.

🔹 **The exoskeleton has numerous segments** running across the structure. These would have allowed the creature to have considerable flexibility.

🔹 **There are large eyes on the head shield**, and short spines, which are often broken off in fossils, extend around the margins of the thorax.

🔹 *Ogyginus* **may have lived** on the seabed, using its eyes to detect moving objects.

🔹 *Trinucleus* **has a very different appearance** from *Ogyginus*, and may have lived in a different habitat.

🔹 **This is a relatively small trilobite**, which grew up to 1.2 in long.

◀ This specimen of Trinucleus shows the deep grooves surrounding the head shield. The long spines extending back from the head shield have broken off.

🔸 **There is a large head shield** with three bulges in it. Around its margin is a fringe with many grooves. Detailed studies suggest that they could have been used to sense changes in water pressure.

🔸 **Complete specimens** of *Trinucleus* have long spines extending from the head shield around the thorax.

Silurian trilobites

- **During the Silurian Period** shallow marine conditions, with reefs, existed at certain times.

- **These reefs** were built up of lime-rich sediment that was bound together by many organisms, including corals and bryozoans. Between the reefs, limestone strata formed.

▶ Trimerus *is a trilobite often found in limestone formed from Silurian reef deposits. In this rich habitat, mollusks, brachiopods, and corals also thrived.*

Conditions at the time were favorable for many different organisms, and these rocks are rich in a variety of fossils. There are brachiopods, corals, mollusks, and trilobites.

Trimerus is an unusual trilobite from Silurian limestone. It has a very smooth carapace (upper exoskeleton), and the three-lobed structure is not easy to see.

The head shield has a triangular outline and there are no eyes.

The smooth exoskeleton and lack of eyes suggest that *Trimerus* may have burrowed into the seabed mud.

Dalmanites was a small Ordovician and Silurian trilobite, which had eyes raised above the head shield.

Trilobites with raised eyes may have had good all-round vision. They may also have burrowed into the mud on the seabed, with their eyes protruding.

Dalmanites has a typical trilobite structure, with three lobes and obvious head, thorax, and tail sections.

In some species of *Dalmanites*, the tail section (pygidium) ends in a sharp spine.

Very small trilobites

Agnostus is one of the earliest trilobites, occurring in strata of Cambrian age.

As well as being a very small trilobite, about 0.4 in long, *Agnostus* has some unusual features.

This trilobite has only two segments making up its thorax. The head shield and tail are both semicircular.

Agnostus had no eyes on the head shield.

In some areas, great masses of broken exoskeletons of *Agnostus* are preserved as fossils.

Some of the most amazing Cambrian fossils come from the Burgess Shale of British Columbia, and from Vastergotland in Sweden. In these areas, masses of strange, soft-bodied creatures and large numbers of crustaceans are preserved. These give us an idea of what life in the Cambrian sea was really like.

DID YOU KNOW?
The predominance of fossil trilobites, including Agnostus, in Cambrian rocks is probably a result of their hard exoskeletons being more easily preserved than the remains of soft-bodied creatures.

Fossils of *Agnostus* have been found rolled up, like woodlice.

In well-preserved fossils from Sweden, *Agnostus* trilobites have been found with an unusual appendage. This has made some paleontologists wonder if *Agnostus* really is a trilobite.

Agnostus **usually occurs** with fossils of other trilobites, mollusks, and graptolites.

▼ *A mass of fragments of* Agnostus *trilobites preserved in limestone. Their typical length was 0.4 in.*

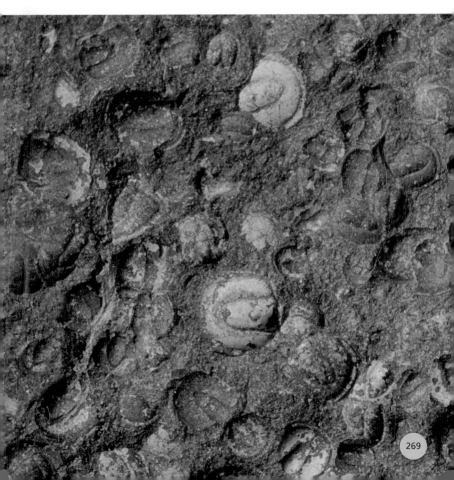

Trilobite vision

🔹 **Trilobites first appeared** in the Cambrian Period and unlike many of the creatures of the time, some were able to see.

🔹 **Fossilized eyes** may seem a little strange, as eyes are soft and decay rapidly after death. Trilobites' eyes, however, were made of calcite (calcium carbonate), and could be easily fossilized.

🔹 **Calcite** is a common mineral, which is found in many rocks, especially limestone. Under the right conditions, it can remain for millions of years in the Earth's crust, without being changed.

🔹 **Trilobites** are related to many modern creatures with excellent eyesight, such as dragonflies, flies, wasps, bees, crabs, and lobsters.

🔹 **Like many modern-day insects**, trilobites had compound eyes.

🔹 **Human eyes** only have one lens, but compound eyes have many lenses all joined together.

■ **Compound eyes** are excellent for seeing movement. For example, modern-day dragonflies can see smaller insects flying nearby and suddenly change direction to catch them.

■ **Scientists** have tried to work out what a trilobite could see with its compound eyes. Many species probably had very good vision.

■ **Some trilobites** had eyes on stalks extending from the head shield. They may have lived on the seabed, with their eyes sticking out of the mud like periscopes.

■ **Not all trilobites had eyes**. Some used feelers and grooves in their exoskeleton for detecting the movement of water currents and finding their way around.

◀ Asaphus, *a type of trilobite, had eyes on raised stalks.*

Continental drift and trilobites

🔹 **The theory of continental drift** suggests that the large land masses (continents) are constantly moving. At times during the past they have been joined together, though now many are separate.

🔹 **A number of fossils** have been used to prove this theory, including the trilobite *Olenellus*. It can help to show that Scotland, U.K., and North America were once joined together.

🔹 **This trilobite** can be found in rocks from the Cambrian Period.

🔹 **During the Cambrian Period**, North America and Scotland, U.K., were joined. A deep ocean separated this area from Wales, U.K., and *Olenellus* was unable to move across it.

🔹 **Although there are many places** where Cambrian trilobites occur in Britain, *Olenellus* is only found in northwest Scotland, U.K.

🔹 *Olenellus* is also fossilized in Cambrian rocks in North America.

🔹 **The rocks** in which *Olenellus* is found were probably formed in relatively shallow marine conditions. These rocks include limestone and mudstone.

🔹 **The main feature** that distinguishes *Olenellus* from other trilobites is its spines, which extend from the head shield and from the sides of the thorax and tail.

🔹 *Olenellus* had large, curved eyes on the sides of the head shield.

🔹 **It is an example** of an advanced Cambrian creature with no obvious ancestors.

▲ *A fossilized*
Olenellus *trilobite*
from Cambrian rocks.

Mollusks

Found in a great variety of habitats, mollusks are very important fossils, occurring as far back as Cambrian times.

Mollusks can live in both salt and fresh water. Some live on land, and some even climb trees. Fossil mollusks are good indicators of the habitat in which a layer of rock was deposited.

The word "mollusk" refers to creatures that have a soft, slimy body, which may or may not have a shell around it.

Mollusks include octopuses, slugs and snails, clams and oysters, squids and cuttlefish, and tusk shells.

Scientifically, the phylum Mollusca is divided into smaller groups called classes. Among the main classes are the Gastropoda, Bivalvia, and Cephalopoda.

Some gastropods (Gastropoda) can live in water and others live on land. They are slugs, snails, and limpets. This class is not as common in the fossil record as the other mollusks.

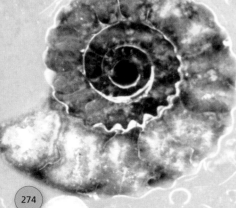

Bivalves (Bivalvia) live in both salt and fresh water. Some bivalves, such as Mya (types of clam), burrow into sand and mud. *Pecten* (the scallop) can open and close its valves to swim, and oysters lie on the seabed.

The **cephalopods** (Cephalopoda) are marine animals. They are among the most intelligent invertebrates, with a well-developed nervous system and sensitive eyes. Octopuses, squid, cuttlefish, and the pearly nautiluses are in this class.

The **ammonites**, one of the best-known groups of fossil, are classified as mollusks, and belong to the class Cephalopoda.

Mollusks are common as fossils, and sometimes occur in such large numbers that they make up most of a sedimentary rock.

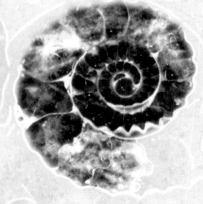

◀ Ammonites are one of the best-known groups of extinct mollusks. They are common in strata of Mesozoic age.

Bivalve mollusks

These mollusks are called bivalves because they have a shell made of two, usually similar, valves, which are a mirror image of each other.

Near the rounded or pointed "beak" of the shell (the umbo), there is a dark, horny, flexible ligament that holds the two valves together.

Just below the umbo, on the insides of the shell, is a series of ridges (teeth) and hollows (sockets). Teeth in one valve fit into sockets in the other valve and, together with the ligament, make a hinge system.

Inside the shell, the animal's body is surrounded by a fleshy membrane called the mantle.

Two strong muscles, the adductor muscles, pull the valves together. When they relax, the valves open slightly.

Features of the many fossil species of bivalves differ, often depending on the habitat in which the creature lived.

◄ This image shows the soft body of a scallop shell between the two valves. When the valves open and close, the animal swims in short bursts.

▲ *This mass of shells is from the early Jurassic Period. They are very like modern scallops, and probably lived in a similar way, opening and closing their valves to swim.*

Pseudopecten, from the Jurassic Period, and the modern Pecten (scallop) have one large adductor muscle. Although they are separated by many millions of years, their features are similar.

These two bivalves open and shut their valves using the large adductor muscle. This causes shellfish to swim in rather jerky movements through the sea.

In fossils and empty modern shells, the point at which the adductor muscle joined the inside of a valve can be seen as a small, rounded indentation. This is the muscle scar.

Pecten has a triangular shell with a pointed umbo. The valves are flat and strengthened with ribs.

Fossil oysters

◀ **From the Mesozoic Era** to recent times, oysters have been common marine shellfish.

◀ **Some fossil oysters** are very similar to those that live today, but others developed rather different shell shapes.

◀ **Unlike most bivalve mollusks**, oysters have valves that are not mirror images of each other. One of the valves is generally larger than the other.

◀ **Oysters** cannot move freely, and live on the seabed. They have many features that help them survive in shallow, turbulent water.

◀ **Usually an oyster** has very thick, heavy valves. These are well adapted to being washed around by currents and tides, without being damaged.

◀ **The adductor muscle** is large and strong to hold the valves together when the shell is moved about by the sea.

◀ The wavy structure on this oyster shell is the edge of its fleshy body. Oysters have to open their shells to feed.

🐚 **As is typical of oysters**, *Gryphaea* had valves that are very different from each other. One valve was large and heavy, the other was thinner and smaller.

🐚 **The larger valve** was hooked at one end and made of many layers of calcite.

🐚 **This structure** probably allowed *Gryphaea* to lie on the seabed, with the heavy valve underneath. If disturbed by water currents, it would come to rest in this position again.

▲ *Gryphaea is a common fossil oyster from the Jurassic Period.*

Cenozoic bivalves

- **Many of the marine bivalve mollusks** that live today evolved during the Cenozoic Era.

- **Most of the shells** found on the beach are bivalve mollusks. Often the more delicate ones are broken, but some, especially those adapted to live on the seabed, may be washed up undamaged.

- *Venericardia*, a type of clam occurs in Paleocene and Eocene strata.

- **This bivalve** lived just below the surface of the mud or sand on the seabed, in a very shallow burrow.

- **It had a massive shell**, with strong ribs running across it to help withstand being disturbed and rolled around by sea currents.

DID YOU KNOW?

During fossilization, especially in shallow water where coarse sediment such as sand is deposited, the strongest shells stand the best chance of being preserved.

🐚 **The wide part** of the shell was in the upper part of the burrow, very near the sediment surface, so that it could feed from the water.

🐚 *Arctica*, a living clam, is similar to *Venericardia*. It has a strong shell adapted to shallow conditions, and lives in a shallow burrow.

🐚 **Although *Arctica*** still survives today, it is also found fossilized in Eocene strata.

🐚 **These two bivalves** rarely occur on their own as fossils. Usually the strata in which they are found contains many other bivalves, gastropods, and fish teeth.

◄ Arctica *is a thick-shelled bivalve found in rocks from the Pliocene Epoch. It still lives today on the continental shelf, burrowing into sand and mud.*

Freshwater bivalves

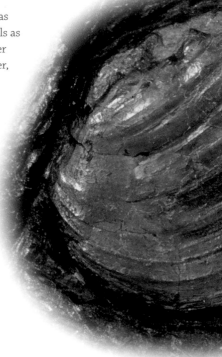

🐚 **Many bivalves** have adapted to living in fresh water. About one fifth of bivalves living today are found in lakes and rivers.

🐚 **In some cases**, where they are isolated geographically from other similar bivalves, new types have evolved.

🐚 **Bivalves** that live in fresh water are different from their marine relatives.

🐚 **Fresh water** does not hold as many shell-making chemicals as sea water does, so freshwater bivalves tend to have thinner, more delicate shells than marine ones.

🐚 **Many different** freshwater bivalves are found fossilized in rocks of Carboniferous age.

🐚 **During the later part** of the Carboniferous Period, much of Europe and North America was covered with river systems and deltas. Bivalve mollusks flourished in the streams and lakes on the deltas.

Carbonicola is a typical inhabitant of Carboniferous waters. It is found fossilized in strata associated with coal beds.

This small bivalve burrowed into the soft mud of streambeds.

Many years ago, coal miners referred to the layers containing *Carbonicola* and other non-marine bivalves as "mussel bands."

Most bivalves are not much use for the relative dating of rock strata. The bivalves that lived in the Carboniferous rivers and swamps can, however, help to link rocks geographically from place to place.

◀ This thin-shelled bivalve lived in streams during the Carboniferous Period.

Fossil gastropods

◀ Straparollus *moved slowly around the seabed, feeding. This specimen is from Carboniferous strata.*

- **Some gastropods**, such as snails, have shells. Others such as slugs have no external shells.

- **Gastropods** have evolved since the Cambrian Period, when they first appear as fossils.

- **Fossil gastropods** are not as common as fossil bivalves and cephalopods.

DID YOU KNOW?

Gastropods such as these are often found fossilized with many other mollusks, brachiopods, and corals. This shows that the habitat on the Paleozoic seabed was favorable to life.

- **There are probably more gastropods** alive today than at any time in the past.

- **Gastropods** have adapted to many habitats. Some live in the sea, both crawling on the seabed and floating as plankton. They are also common on dry land.

- *Poleumita* is a typical sea snail from Silurian marine strata.

- **This gastropod** occurs in limestones deposited in shallow water, including those formed on reefs.

- *Poleumita* has a shell that coils in a low spiral. There are ridges and small spines on the shell.

- *Straparollus* lived from the Silurian to Permian Periods. It had a fairly smooth shell and lived in shallow seas.

Cenozoic gastropods

- **During the Cenozoic Era**, gastropods began to develop different groups that still live today.

- **Fossil gastropods** often have their original shell intact, showing as much detail as a modern shell found on the beach.

- **Though fossils** of *Turritella* first occurred in rocks of Cretaceous age, it evolved into a number of species during the Cenozoic Era.

- ***Turritella***, also known as towershell or turretshell, has a long, narrow shell with screwlike coiling. The fossil species are closely related to modern tower screw shells.

- **The coils** of the shell are called whorls. *Turritella* has a groove between each whorl.

- **The only details** on the shell are faint growth lines, which mark an earlier position of the shell opening.

- **Like many gastropods**, *Turritella* lived in shallow seas, and is found fossilized with other mollusks, corals, and crustaceans.

- **Masses of *Turritella* shells** sometimes appear together, and make up a high percentage of the rock.

- **Modern species** of *Turritella* usually burrow into the mud and silt on the seabed. The sharp end of the shell points downward and the opening is near the surface of the seabed.

- **It is probable that fossil gastropods** lived in a similar way. For them to be fossilized in large numbers, they must have been disturbed by sea currents and the shells washed together.

▶ *This mass of perfectly preserved* Turritella *shells is from Eocene strata in France.*

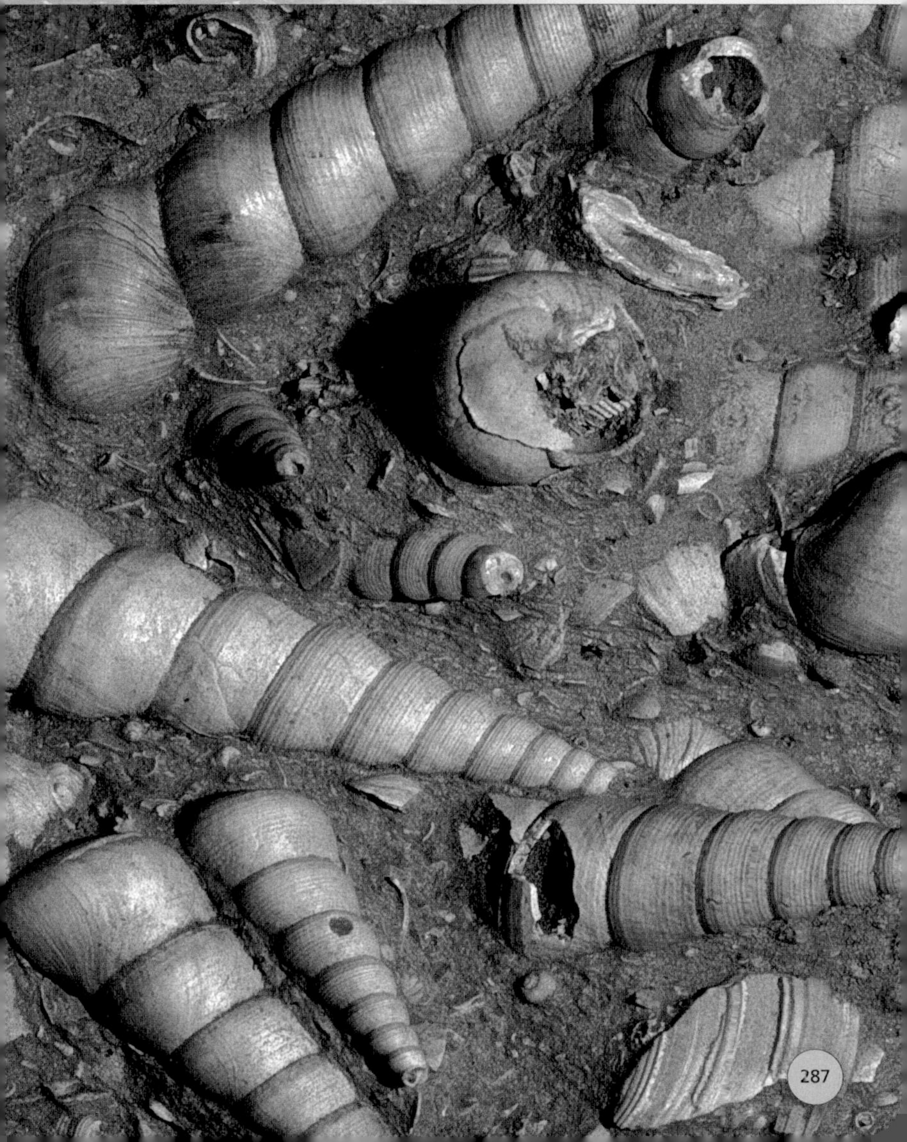

Predatory sea snails

- **During the Cretaceous Period**, gastropod mollusks were not as common as other groups, but in the Cenozoic Era they evolved rapidly.

- **Marine gastropods** developed many ways of feeding. Some became active predators.

- **Almost half** the number of fossilized gastropods found in rocks of Eocene age were predators.

- **These sea snails** were not very big, and many of them had sophisticated ways of killing and eating their prey.

DID YOU KNOW?

Conus has a highly advanced radula that was like a thin harpoon. This was stuck into prey and then venom injected through a groove in the radula.

- **Almost anything** living on the seabed would have been attacked by these snails. Sea urchins, mollusks, and worms were all eaten. Some species even caught live fish.

- *Conus*, the cone shell, was a typical predatory gastropod from the Eocene Epoch.

- **This small sea snail** had a very ornate shell, crossed by sharp ridges and lines. It is often fossilized in large masses.

- **Gastropods** have a radula for feeding. The radula is a sharp "tongue" that is used to attack prey or rasp off plant material.

- *Conus* is found fossilized with many other mollusks, fish teeth, echinoids, and corals.

◄ This modern cone shell shoots its poisonous radula into a whelk's shell. The venom is very powerful and quickly paralyzes the prey.

Cephalopods

- **This class of mollusks** contains some of the most advanced invertebrates to have ever evolved.

- **The pearly nautilus**, octopus, squid, and cuttlefish are all cephalopods, as well as many extinct groups such as ammonites and belemnites.

- **Modern cephalopods** have a highly developed nervous system and good eyesight.

- **All these creatures** live in the sea, and most are capable of free movement, often by jet propulsion.

- **As well as** squirting water for propulsion, many cephalopods can emit a cloud of dark, inky liquid, behind which they can hide from predators.

- **Both the external** and internal shells of cephalopods are common as fossils.

◀ These cephalopods (Orthoceras) are from Ordovician rocks. They are straight-shelled nautiloids, and the buoyancy chambers can be seen where the shell has broken off.

▶ The modern octopus is a free-swimming mollusk that lacks an outer shell. It is a very advanced animal, with a complex nervous system and good eyesight.

Orthoceras is an early, straight-shelled nautilus, from lower Paleozoic strata. The shell, like that of many cephalopods, is divided into chambers, with the animal living in the largest one at the open end of the shell.

Some species of *Orthoceras* grew to several feet in length, though most were only a few inches long.

In some areas, such as the limestone at Maquokota in Illinois, U.S., large numbers of *Orthoceras* are found fossilized together.

Specimens of *Orthoceras* limestone containing these fossils are cut and polished for ornamental use.

Devonian and Carboniferous cephalopods

Suture line

- **In the upper Paleozoic Era**, especially during the Devonian and Carboniferous periods, cephalopods evolved with coiled external shells.

- **The coiled shell** had many chambers. At the wide end of the shell was the body chamber in which the squidlike animal lived.

- **Many smaller buoyancy chambers** extended back from the body chamber to the tightly coiled center of the shell.

- **These chambers** may have been crushed on bedding planes during fossilization. In many cases however, they are preserved and infilled with crystals of minerals such as calcite.

🔹 **Some cephalopod shells** are similar to a coil of rope, with all the coils (whorls) easily seen. This is called evolute coiling.

🔹 **Shells** where the whorls overlap a great deal are said to have involute coiling.

🔹 **The goniatites** are a group of cephalopods that lived in the sea during the Devonian and Carboniferous periods.

🔹 **Goniatites** may have been the ancestors of the Mesozoic ammonites and generally had involute shells.

🔹 **The suture lines** have a zigzag pattern and mark where the walls of the internal buoyancy chambers meet the outer shell.

🔹 **The common**, free-swimming goniatites are used as zone fossils for marine strata of Devonian and Carboniferous age.

◀ *Goniatites are small cephalopods. The zigzag suture pattern is clearly seen in this example from the Carboniferous Period.*

Modern and Jurassic nautilus

🐚 **The pearly nautilus**, which today lives in the southwestern Pacific Ocean mainly around Australia and Indonesia, is regarded as a "living fossil."

🐚 **Fossils** of similar species of nautilus occur in rocks dating back to the early Mesozoic Era.

🐚 *Nautilus* has a broad shell with involute coiling. The inner whorls are largely hidden by the large outermost whorl.

🐚 *Cenoceras* was a Jurassic nautilus, with many features similar to the modern pearly nautilus.

🐚 **The suture lines** on a nautilus shell are gently curved, not zigzagged as in the goniatites, or complex as in the ammonites.

🐚 **Like many shelled cephalopods**, *Nautilus* has a large body chamber. The squidlike animal has numerous tentacles, eyes, and a funnel for squirting water, providing jet propulsion.

🐚 **The smaller buoyancy chambers** are linked through their centers by a thin tube—the siphuncle. This allows the density of fluid and gas in the chambers to be regulated.

◀ Cenoceras *had a large body chamber, and the inner coils of the shell are covered by the large outermost coil.*

▶ *The modern nautilus lives in the western Pacific Ocean, especially around Australia. It has good eyesight and moves by squirting out a jet of water.*

🐚 **The nautilus** has many biological differences from the extinct ammonites. However its shell is similar and may give a good insight into how ammonites lived.

🐚 **Because fossilized** nautilus shells span such a long period of time, they are little use as zone fossils.

🐚 **Nautilus shells** are found washed ashore in east Africa and Madagascar, many hundreds of miles from where they live. Shells of dead ammonites could probably have drifted across the Mesozoic sea, thus enhancing their use as zone fossils.

Ammonites

🐚 **During the Jurassic and Cretaceous periods**, ammonites evolved into a great variety of forms.

🐚 **Ammonites** were marine creatures, and many could move freely in the water. Some of the largest may have browsed on the seabed.

🐚 **The ammonite shell** is similar to the nautilus shell, but there are some very important differences.

🐚 **The spiral coiling** of the ammonite shell does not extend upward. It is coiled in a flat plane, with both sides depressed in the center.

🐚 **An ammonite shell** has a large body chamber at the shell opening. This chamber reaches back for about half a whorl. Usually the animal lived with the body chamber at the lowest point, and the rest of the shell above.

🐚 **The smaller buoyancy chambers** are linked by a thin tube, called the siphuncle. This runs along the outside of each whorl, not in the center as in the nautilus.

🐚 **The buoyancy chambers** are separated from each other by walls called septa. Where these reach the shell, they become very complex. If some of the outer shell is worn away, or removed, these complex patterns are revealed as suture lines.

🐚 **Ammonite shells** can be distinguished from nautilus and goniatite shells by their wavy, frilly, or lobed suture lines.

🐚 *Psiloceras* is one of the first ammonites to appear in rocks of Jurassic age. As ammonites are used as zone fossils, it marks the base of the Jurassic Period.

🐚 **This ammonite** has a shell coiled mid-way between involute and evolute, and only faint ridges running across the whorls.

1. Whorl

2. Frilly suture lines

3. Body chamber

▶ It is unusual to
find uncrushed
specimens of Psiloceras.
These examples are from
a boulder washed up on the
shore of North Yorkshire, U.K.

Ammonite variety and movement

- **Fossil ammonite shells** show a vast range of different shapes, sizes, and structures. The movement of different species may have depended on their shape.

- **Some ammonites** were big and round, others were thin and disk-shaped. Some had shells that were quite small; others were large.

- **The outer surface** of a fossil ammonite shell may be covered with ridges (ribs), spines, and knobs.

- **Exactly** what function these features had is unknown. Ribs may have added strength to the shell, and spines may have helped protect against predators.

- **For an animal** that was able to swim, various features of the shell could have kept the ammonite in the correct position and helped with streamlining.

- **Scientists** have studied how the nautilus moves in order to try to suggest the swimming ability of ammonites.

▶ *This reconstruction shows the ammonite* Lytoceras *swimming in the warm Jurassic ocean. Ammonites had far fewer tentacles than the nautilus.*

Base of the spines

▶ *Only the base of the spines remain on the shell of this fossil* Liparoceras. *The specimen comes from early Jurassic strata.*

🐚 **Nautiluses** can move both slowly and in rapid bursts by using the muscles in its large body cavity, and by squirting water from its funnel.

🐚 **Ammonites** had a very different body chamber from that of the nautilus. In the ammonite shell, the part occupied by the animal's body was narrow and tube-shaped, though some did have wide body chambers. The nautilus has a wide, expanded body chamber.

🐚 **It is thought that** most ammonites were poor swimmers, especially when compared with modern squids.

🐚 **By altering the fluids and gas** in the buoyancy chambers, ammonites could regulate their density, and were able to change their depth in the water.

Ammonite suture lines

- **One of the most** striking features of fossil ammonites is the pattern of complex lines that can often be seen running across the shell. These are called suture lines.

- **The suture lines** do not occur on the outside of the shell, and must not be confused with the ribs or other external markings.

- **Suture lines** are on the inner surface of the shell. Only slightly worn shells, or shells where some of the outermost material is broken off, show these complex lines.

- **Each suture line** marks where an internal division between two chambers joined the inner surface of the shell.

- **This join** was very complicated, as shown by the pattern of the suture line.

▲ When polished, and the outer layer of shell removed from this Eparietites, *the intricate suture lines can be clearly seen.*

▼ Baculites *is an uncoiled ammonite from Cretaceous rocks. The very complex suture lines are typical of this genus.*

Ammonite fossils often break, and a small fossil may be only the inner whorls of a large ammonite. The body chamber and large outer whorls would have been destroyed.

It is easy to tell if an ammonite specimen is complete by looking at the suture lines.

In a complete ammonite shell, there are no suture lines for the first half whorl. This is where the undivided body chamber is. The suture lines only begin where the buoyancy chambers are.

Suture patterns vary greatly between ammonites. All are very complicated. Some have rounded shapes, some spiky patterns, and others are wavy.

Ammonites are frequently sold as ornaments. Often these are highly polished and the outer shell removed, to show the amazing suture patterns.

Giant ammonites

- **Ammonite shells** vary greatly in size. The majority are a few inches in diameter, and some are much larger.

- **In order to study** ammonite shells and determine the average size of different species, certain rules have to be followed.

- **A lack of suture lines** near the shell opening shows that the body chamber is present. The shell will be complete if this is the case.

- **Paleontologists** also have certain ways of telling if an ammonite is a small juvenile.

- **Mature shells** often have widened shell openings and the last few sutures crowd together.

- **One of the largest ammonites** is aptly named *Titanites*. It could grow to about 3 ft in diameter.

- *Titanites* occurs in late Jurassic rocks. It is loosely coiled and has strong ribs crossing the shell.

- **An even larger ammonite** is *Parapuzosia,* from late Cretaceous strata, which grew to 8.2 ft in diameter.

- **It is probable** that such large ammonites lived near, or on, the seabed, rather than swimming freely.

DID YOU KNOW?
Before measuring the size of a fossilized ammonite shell, it is important to make sure it is complete. This is done by examining the shell carefully and looking for the suture lines.

◄ *This specimen of
Titanites is just under 3 ft
in diameter. It is on
display in the Geology
Department at the
University of Keele,
Staffordshire, U.K.*

Tit nites titan e.s. BUCKMAN 1921
UPPER JURASSIC PORTLANDIAN STAGE.
DORSET. ENGLAND.
"TYPE MMONITES" VOL.III. PLATE CCXXXI
PRESENTED BY H.M. GEOLOGICAL SURVEY

Ammonites as zone fossils

Zone fossils help paleontologists to put strata into sequences. They also allow strata to be linked, or correlated, from place to place.

For a fossil group to be chosen for this work, it must have certain features. Ammonites are probably the best zone fossils, as they have nearly all the requirements.

A relative time zone should be as short as possible. This allows very precise dating of rocks. It is not much use having a time zone tens of millions of years long. Far too many rocks form in such a huge expanse of time, and correlating them would be too difficult.

The ammonite species chosen as zone fossils represent small parts of geological time.

Ammonites evolved rapidly into many species. Each species lived for a short time before becoming extinct.

Because ammonites lived in the sea and could move about, certain species are found in many different regions. They are useful in correlating strata from place to place.

◄▼ Asteroceras is known from many parts of the world in Jurassic strata. "Asteroceras" means "star horn."

🐚 **Shells of dead ammonites** could drift on ocean currents, as modern nautilus shells do, and be carried to distant places.

🐚 **A zone fossil** should be easily fossilized. A jellyfish may have all the attributes required for correlating rocks, but it is rarely found as a fossil. Ammonite shells are easily preserved.

🐚 **It is important** for a zone fossil to be common. Field geologists need to be able to find them to do their work. Ammonites are numerous in Jurassic and Cretaceous rocks, and these periods are zoned by ammonites.

🐚 **Because of their varied structures**, it is easy to tell one zone ammonite from another, making that part of the geological time scale easy to work out.

Uncoiled ammonites

▲ *This uncoiled* Spiroceras *shell has many ammonite features. There are ribs, and the shell tapers at one end.*

◀ **The classic ammonite shell** is coiled in a flat spiral. Some shells have a large body chamber that overlaps the smaller, inner whorls.

◀ **During ammonite evolution**, many different shells appeared that initially don't look like ammonites.

At many times during the Jurassic and Cretaceous periods, some ammonite species developed uncoiled shells.

One of the strangest of these is *Didymoceras,* which occurs in the Cretaceous rocks of Colorado, U.S.

This ammonite is the corkscrew shape of a ram's horn, coiled in a very open spiral.

Many uncoiled ammonites have a more U-shaped structure, such as *Hamites,* from the Cretaceous Period.

Spiroceras is from Jurassic strata. By uncoiling, it has lost the classic ammonite symmetry.

Spiroceras retains some ammonite features, such as the thick ribs that run across the shell.

Uncoiled ammonites were probably poorer swimmers than their coiled relatives. An uncoiled shell would not be as stable, and these ammonites may have moved slowly along the seabed, feeding.

DID YOU KNOW?
Toward the end of their evolution, in the late Cretaceous Period, uncoiling was common. Other strange shapes also appeared at this time.

Cretaceous ammonites

- **During the Cretaceous Period**, ammonites flourished and many new shell shapes evolved.

- **Some Cretaceous ammonites** were uncoiled, with straight shells. Others were curved, and almost U-shaped.

- *Baculites*, a straight Cretaceous ammonite, is well-known for its remarkable pattern of suture lines.

- **This ammonite** is common in Cretaceous rocks in South Dakota, U.S. It grew to a great size, reaching up to 6.5 ft in length.

- *Scaphites* is a partly uncoiled ammonite from the Cretaceous Period.

- **The body chamber** of *Scaphites* is large and uncoiled. An ammonite with this structure was probably not adapted to swimming. It more likely lived on, or near the seabed, with the shell opening slightly upward.

- *Douvilleiceras* is a Cretaceous ammonite, with the usual ammonite coiling. It had rows of large knobs running around the shell.

🐚 **This ammonite** is widespread and common in Cretaceous rocks, and is used as a zone fossil for this period.

🐚 *Mantelliceras* lived in the Cretaceous sea, on the bed that chalk was being deposited on. It had strong ribs running across its shell.

🐚 **At the end** of the Cretaceous Period, ammonites became extinct. The exact reasons for this are unknown, although they had been declining in numbers of genera for some time. At the same time, many other groups of animals, both on land (for example, the dinosaurs) and in the sea (75 percent of marine plankton) died out.

▲ This dusty, white specimen of Douvilleiceras is found in upper Cretaceous rocks, where chalk is the dominant rock.

Ammonites with beaks

🐚 **Certain ammonites** have a strange beaklike structure on the front of the shell. This is called a lappet.

🐚 *Kosmoceras* is a small ammonite that is well-known for this lappet structure.

🐚 **In the clay strata** where these ammonite shells occur, they are usually crushed flat, but original shell material is often preserved.

🐚 **Much larger** forms of *Kosmoceras* are found fossilized with the smaller shells.

🐚 **Paleontologists** studying both of these ammonites discovered that changes in their shells occurred at the same time. When a new feature developed on the small shell, the same feature appeared on the larger shell.

🐚 **This side-by-side evolution** of two ammonites, one larger than the other, has been found to occur with other species.

Lappet

🔹 **Paleontologists** have analyzed hundreds of specimens of *Kosmoceras* in order to try to understand the evolution of the two size forms of the ammonite.

🔹 **It is believed** that the large and small *Kosmoceras* may be the male and the female of the same species. This would explain their simultaneous evolutionary changes. The sexes of many modern cephalopods have a distinct size difference.

🔹 **The exact purpose** of the lappet on the smaller fossil shell is unknown. Some paleontologists suggest that the small shell was the male and the lappet was a display device.

◀ *This specimen of* Kosmoceras, *with its lappet intact, is from Middle Jurassic strata.*

Fossil squids

- **Squids are cephalopods** with an internal shell. These shells are common fossils in Mesozoic sedimentary strata.

- **The fossilized** internal shells of cephalopods are similar to squid and are called belemnites.

- **Belemnites first appear** as fossils in rocks of the Carboniferous Period, and became extinct early in the Cenozoic Era.

- **The long**, **bullet-shaped fossil**, varying in length from less than half an inch to 6 in or more, is called the guard.

- **As well as the narrow**, tapering part of the shell, there is a much wider, chambered part, called the phragmocone. This fits into the wider end of the guard.

- **Belemnites** are solid objects, made of layers of calcite, so they usually retain their three-dimensional shape when fossilized.

Guard

- **Where masses of belemnites occur** on rock surfaces, they are often all parallel to each other. This suggests that they were moved by seabed currents.

- **The belemnite's soft body** was like that of a typical squid, with tentacles, eyes, and a funnel for squirting water or ink.

- **Belemnites** were probably free-swimming, rather like modern squid, although modern squid have not evolved from them.

- **Fossil belemnite ink sacs** have been found in Jurassic strata. In the 19th century, paleontologists reconstituted the "ink" and used it for writing.

▼ This is an unusual belemnite fossil, as the crushed phragmocone is preserved with the narrow, tapering guard.

Phragmocone

Tusk shells

◀ **Tusk shells** are alive today and are mollusks that belong to a class called the scaphopods. The earliest tusk shells occur in rocks of Ordovician age.

◀ **A scaphopod shell** is a thin tube that is open at each end.

◀ **The name** "tusk shell" describes the way many of these shells curve and taper like an elephant's tusk.

◀ **Modern tusk shells** give many clues as to how prehistoric species may have lived. Today, tusk shells live in shallow seas, mainly on the continental shelf.

◀ **The animal burrows** at a shallow angle into the seabed sediment, and pulls itself down using a muscular foot.

◀ **Its head** is in the deepest part of the burrow. The narrow end of the shell, containing the anus, projects a short distance above the seabed.

◀ **Using specially adapted tentacles**, the tusk shell feeds on minute organisms living in the mud on the seabed.

- **Fossil tusk shells** are often well preserved. When the creature died, the hollow shell could easily fill with mud. This would prevent it from being crushed.

- **_Dentalium_** is found in rocks ranging in age from Cretaceous to Recent. It has changed little in many tens of million of years.

DID YOU KNOW?

Fossil tusk shells have been used by people through the ages for necklaces, nose piercings, and as currency for trading.

◀ These broken tusk shells, Dentalium, are from strata of the Miocene epoch in Tuscany, Italy.

Vertebrate fossils

🔹 **Vertebrates** are creatures that have internal skeletons usually made of bone or cartilage and incorporating a backbone. They include fish, amphibians, reptiles, birds, and mammals.

🔹 **For many reasons**, the fossils of vertebrates are not as common as those of shellfish, arthropods, corals, and other invertebrates.

🔹 **Creatures with backbones** evolved much later than most invertebrates. While trilobites and brachiopods were being fossilized in the Cambrian and Ordovician periods, there were no vertebrates.

▼ Cephalaspis *was an early fossil fish from Devonian strata. Many early fish, including* Cephalaspis, *lived in freshwater lakes.*

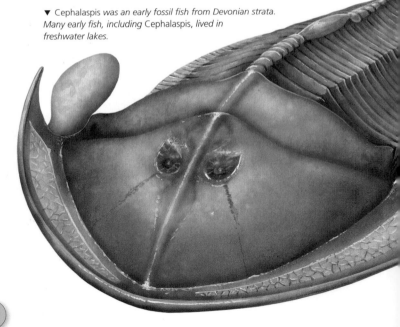

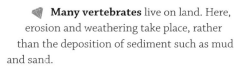

Many vertebrates live on land. Here, erosion and weathering take place, rather than the deposition of sediment such as mud and sand.

The remains of a vertebrate will probably decay and be broken up, rather than be covered with fossilizing sediment.

Many vertebrate fossils are broken and scattered bones, rather than whole skeletons.

There are, however, many excellent cases of masses of vertebrates, including dinosaurs, being fossilized in deposits formed on land, such as those in China and North America.

Fish were the first vertebrates to evolve. Because they live in water, many of them are fossilized.

Cephalaspis was a primitive fish from the Devonian Period.

The large head shield of the *Cephalaspis* had eye sockets on the top, and the mouth was underneath.

DID YOU KNOW?
Like the modern lamprey, Cephalaspis had a suckerlike mouth rather than true jaws.

Early fossil fish

- **Vertebrate evolution** took a great step forward when fish began to survive, even for a short period of time, out of the water.

- **The Devonian continent** was dry and mountainous, but there were great inland freshwater lakes teeming with fish.

- **The remains** of many of these fish are preserved in the muddy sandstone that formed on the lakebeds.

- **Fish** living in freshwater ponds and lakes are often fossilized in large numbers. If part of the lake system dries up, many fish die.

- **Fish scales** are very durable and are easily preserved as fossils.

- *Dipterus* was one of the many different fish that lived in Devonian lakes.

▼ Dipterus *is a fossil fish that lived in freshwater lakes during the Devonian Period. It could have possibly survived out of water for some time.*

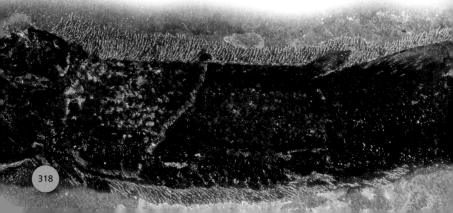

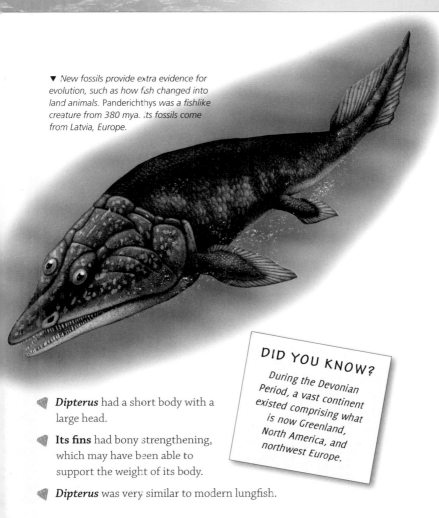

▼ New fossils provide extra evidence for evolution, such as how fish changed into land animals. Panderichthys was a fishlike creature from 380 mya. Its fossils come from Latvia, Europe.

DID YOU KNOW?

During the Devonian Period, a vast continent existed comprising what is now Greenland, North America, and northwest Europe.

◀ *Dipterus* had a short body with a large head.

◀ **Its fins** had bony strengthening, which may have been able to support the weight of its body.

◀ *Dipterus* was very similar to modern lungfish.

319

Armored fish

🐚 *Bothriolepis* comes from the renowned fossil site of Miguasha near Scaumenac Bay in Canada.

🐚 **Fossils** were first discovered at this now famous site in the mid-19th century.

🐚 **The rocks** there contain thousands of exceptionally well-preserved fossils of fish and other organisms.

🐚 **These remarkable** numbers of fine fossils have attracted both professional and amateur collectors.

DID YOU KNOW?

In order to prevent fossil collectors from ravaging the site, the Miguasha National Park was set up in 1985. In 1999 it became a world heritage site. Any new finds are kept in the museum there.

- **Early fish** were often covered with large scales and armor for protection.

- *Bothriolepis* had a large head shield, which is the only part usually fossilized.

- **The head shield** was heavily armored and covered with rough, bony plates.

- **Extending from each side** of the head were two long, narrow, finlike projections.

- **Paleontologists** have cut many of the well-preserved fossils from Miguasha into sections. They discovered internal details such as two large sacs leading from the pharynx (throat). These may have been lungs.

◀ Only the heavily armored head shield and armlike projections of this Bothriolepis have been preserved.

The Green River fish

- **Exceptional numbers** of fossil fish are preserved in the Green River strata of Wyoming, Colorado and Utah, U.S.

- **These rocks** are limestones formed in the Eocene Epoch.

- **It seems that** during Eocene times, a number of large lakes existed in the Green River region.

- **Fossil pollen** found in the strata shows that dense vegetation grew around the lakes.

- **Many different genera** of fish lived in the Green River area. Fossils of *Knightia, Diplomystus, Gosuitichthys,* and *Priscacara* are all common.

- **Small rock slabs** covered with some of these fish are sold in fossil shops.

▲ Knightia *is one of many fish species preserved in the famous Green River strata.*

- **The climate** in the Green River region was probably warm with definite seasons, during the Eocene Epoch.

- **In the drier season**, the lakes became smaller, and many fish died and became fossilized as the lakes dried up.

- *Gosuitichthys* is in many ways a modern fish, with its backbone near the dorsal surface and masses of ribs supporting the body.

- **Many of the Green River** fossil fish are perfectly preserved, but some are in small pieces. This may be because they exploded during decomposition.

◄ When water in one of the Green River lakes dried up, this mass of Gosuitichthys died, and was covered with mud.

Fossil fish teeth

▼ *This fossil tooth is from an extinct type of* Carcharodon, *which grew far larger than today's great white shark.*

Fish teeth are made of very durable material, and are often the only part of the creature that becomes fossilized.

In some strata formed during the Cenozoic Era, there are large numbers of fossil fish teeth, especially those of sharks.

Many sharks do not have true bony skeletons, and their teeth are all that remain as fossils.

By comparing fossil fish teeth with those of modern fish, it is usually possible to say what the ancient fish were like.

Two fossil sharks that are known mainly from their teeth are *Lamna* and *Odontaspis*.

These sharks were medium-sized predators that grew to about 13 ft in length.

- **The genus *Carcharodon*** is one of the best-known fossil sharks. It also includes today's great white shark.

- **Fossil *Carcharodon*** teeth sometimes called *Carcharodon megalodon*, can be as long as 6 in and occur in Cenozoic strata.

- **From the large size** of the teeth, it seems that this shark may have grown to more than 20 ft in length.

- **The teeth** of *Carcharodon* are triangular in shape, with rows of sharp serrations along their edges.

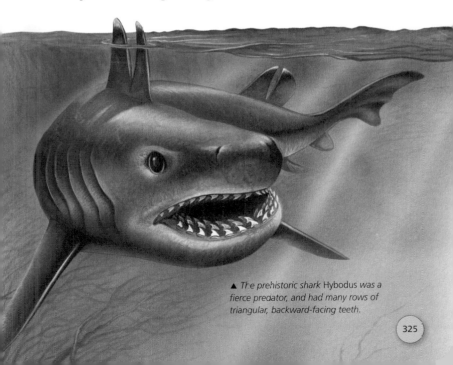

▲ *The prehistoric shark* Hybodus *was a fierce predator, and had many rows of triangular, backward-facing teeth.*

325

Early amphibians

- **The earliest fossil amphibians** are found in rocks of the Devonian age.

- **The first amphibians** probably evolved from fish, such as lungfish, which are similar to *Dipterus*.

- **Modern amphibians** depend on water for survival. Most lay their eggs in water, and their young live in water before being able to breathe air and live on land.

- **Temnospondyls** are a group of early amphibians. Their fossils occur in Carboniferous and younger rocks.

- **With a bony skeleton** and limbs, temnospondyls share many features with modern amphibians.

▶ This fossil temnospondyl (primitive amphibian) is from Odenheim, Germany. Only a gray outline of its body remains, with black carbon traces of the skeleton. It resembles today's newts and salamanders.

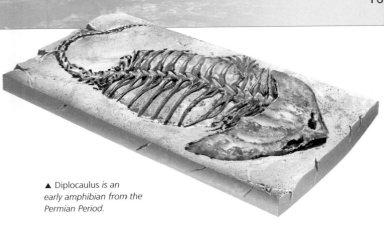

▲ Diplocaulus *is an early amphibian from the Permian Period.*

🔸 **Temnospondyls** had a flexible body, which was probably well-adapted to moving in damp habitats.

🔸 **In West Lothian**, Scotland, virtually complete temnospondyl skeletons have been found in Carboniferous rock.

🔸 **The late Carboniferous swamps** were an ideal habitat for amphibians.

🔸 **As well as** temnospondyl fossils, the Scottish late Carboniferous rocks contain fossils of scorpions, myriapods, and spiders. These are mainly land-dwelling creatures.

🔸 **Reptiles** evolved from amphibians during the Carboniferous Period.

Mosasaurus

- **During the Mesozoic Era**, reptiles developed into many different types, some living on land and others in the sea.

- **The Mesozoic sea** teemed with life, and giant sea reptiles preyed on fish, mollusks, and other invertebrates.

- *Mosasaurus* was a large marine reptile (about 50 ft long) that lived during the Cretaceous Period.

- **Often only its sharp teeth** are fossilized. These are more than 2 in long and they curve to a sharp point.

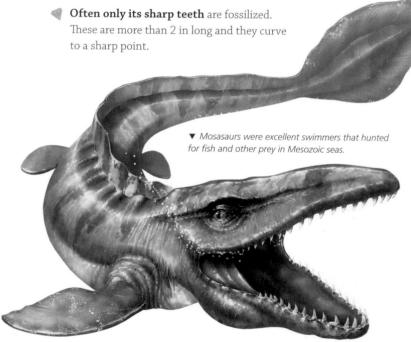

▼ *Mosasaurs were excellent swimmers that hunted for fish and other prey in Mesozoic seas.*

▲ These vertebrae and ribs of a fossil mosasaur are from Cretaceous rocks in France.

- *Mosasaurus* fossils have been found in North America and Northern Europe.

- **The body** of *Mosasaurus* was slender, and it used its powerful tail to propel itself through the water.

- **A study of *Mosasaurus* skulls** has shown that there are many similarities with those of monitor lizards, which live today.

- **Most mosasaurs** probably caught vertebrate prey, including fish. Some had teeth adapted for crushing.

- **The first *Mosasaurus*** remains were found in 1770 in the Netherlands. When first discovered, nobody knew what the giant fossil jaws were.

- **The name *Mosasaurus*** refers to the Meuse region in the Netherlands, where the remains were found.

Pliosaurus and Plesiosaurus

⬤ **The fossilized** bones of *Plesiosaurus* and *Pliosaurus* are not uncommon in Mesozoic strata.

⬤ **The lower Jurassic rocks** at Lyme Regis, Dorset, U.K., have been a well-known fossil site since the early 19th century. Even today, fossil collectors scour the rocks exposed on the shore.

⬤ **The first** *Plesiosaurus* was found at Lyme Regis by Mary Anning in 1821.

⬤ *Plesiosaurus* grew to around 40 ft in length, and its most notable feature was its long neck.

⬤ **The body** of *Plesiosaurus* was short and stout, with four large paddle-shaped limbs.

⬤ *Plesiosaurus* had a small head, and its jaw was filled with many sharp teeth.

⬤ **It may have fed** by slinging its head at prey using its long, flexible neck.

- **Pliosaurus** was very similar to *Plesiosaurus*, but had a much shorter neck with a large head.

- **It probably hunted** live prey including reptiles, fish, and mollusks such as ammonites.

▲ *This short-necked pliosaur was an active hunter in the Jurassic seas.*

Ichthyosaurus

- **Fossils** of *Ichthyosaurus* have been known since the beginning of the 19th century.

- **These fossil marine reptiles** are found in rocks of Triassic, Jurassic, and Cretaceous age.

- *Ichthyosaurus* lacked the long neck of *Plesiosaurus,* and had a long, beaklike snout.

- **The mouth** was filled with conical, grooved teeth, designed for tearing prey apart.

- **The body of *Ichthyosaurus*** was streamlined, with a large, pointed dorsal fin and powerful front paddle fins. The rear pair of fins was much smaller.

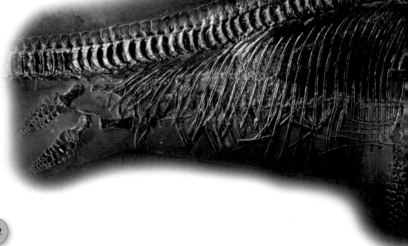

- **The tail had bones** in only the lower part, and would have probably moved the animal upward as well as forward in the water.

- **Many remarkable** fossil ichthyosaurs have been found. Whole skeletons surrounded by a black impression of the body, including details of the paddles and tail, occur in Germany.

- **Fossils have proved** that *Ichthyosaurus* gave birth to live young. At least one adult skeleton has been found with a juvenile skeleton inside it.

- **Cephalopods**, including ammonites, had hooks on their tentacles. One *Ichthyosaurus* stomach contained the hooks from at least 1,600 cephalopods.

◄ This ichthyosaur's skeleton shows a strong spine that allowed the body to bend during movement in the water. The large eye sockets indicate good vision.

DID YOU KNOW?
An Ichthyosaurus that died giving birth has been fossilized, with the baby skeleton protruding from the birth canal.

Dinosaurs

▼ *A reconstruction of a Cretaceous scene.*

1	*Edmontonia*
2	*Triceratops*
3	*Avimimus*
4	*Lambeosaurus*
5	*Struthiomimus*
6	*Albertosaurus*
7	*Corythosaurus*
8	*Parasaurolophus*
9	*Euoplocephalus*
10	*Tyrannosaurus*

- **The dinosaurs** were a group of reptiles that evolved during the Mesozoic Era (248–65 mya). The name dinosaur means "terrible lizard."

- **All dinosaurs** lived on land. Some may have wandered into freshwater swamps, but none lived in the sea.

- **Dinosaurs** are classified in a group of reptiles called archosaurs.

- **Other archosaurs** include crocodiles and the extinct pterosaurs.

- **Dinosaurs** were a very varied and successful group. They lived for around 165 million years, before becoming extinct at the end of the Cretaceous Period.

- **Some dinosaurs,** such as *Diplodocus* were enormous and slow moving. Others, such as *Compsognathus*, were small and nimble.

- **Many dinosaurs** laid eggs, from which their young hatched. Dinosaur nests have been found, including those of *Protocerotops* in Mongolia.

- **Dinosaurs** evolved to live in many habitats and to eat different food. *Allosaurus* was a predatory carnivore (meat eater) and *Stegosaurus* was a herbivore (plant eater).

- **There are many theories** about dinosaurs extinction. It is probable that a giant meteorite hit Earth in Mexico. This would have altered the climate and destroyed food chains.

- **Perhaps dinosaurs** are not extinct. Birds are thought to have evolved from dinosaurs, and may simply be modern, feathered versions of the prehistoric reptiles.

Stegosaurus

◀ *Stegosaurus* lived during the late Jurassic Period (160–145 mya).

◀ **It was a relatively large dinosaur**, with adults growing to about 30 ft in length, and possibly weighing up to 2 tons.

◀ **Fossils** of *Stegosaurus* come mainly from the western parts of North America, especially Wyoming, Utah, and Colorado. Relatives of *Stegosaurus* such as *Kentrosaurus* have been found fossilized in South East Africa and fossils of *Tujiangosaurus* have been found in East Asia.

◀ *Stegosaurus* was a thick-set dinosaur that walked on all four legs.

◀ **Along its back**, *Stegosaurus* had a double row of large, relatively flat, bony plates.

◀ **The tail** of *Stegosaurus* was heavy and thick where it joined the body. It tapered rapidly to a point, and at the end it had four large bony spikes.

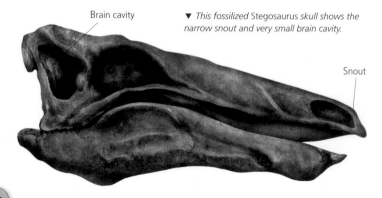

Brain cavity

▼ *This fossilized* Stegosaurus *skull shows the narrow snout and very small brain cavity.*

Snout

▲ Stegosaurus *had a tiny head in comparison to its body. Its brain was tiny, too, indicating a lack of intelligence.*

There are a number of theories as to the function of the bony plates. They may have contained blood vessels, and so adjusted body temperature.

The bony plates could have been held flat against the body as a means of defense, and the tail spikes may have been used to swing at attackers.

Stegosaurus had a very small head. The mouth had tiny serrated teeth. It is possible that food was broken down by stones in its stomach, which the animal swallowed, rather than by its teeth.

Stegosaurus **moved slowly**, and fed on vegetation. It would probably have been preyed on by carnivores such as *Allosaurus*.

Triceratops

- **Triceratops** lived around 70 to 65 mya, during the late Cretaceous Period. It was one of the last dinosaurs.

- **The name _Triceratops_** means "three-horned face."

- **Most of the fossils** of _Triceratops_ have been found in central North America, in Montana, North and South Dakota, and Wyoming. Fossils have also been found in Alberta and Saskatchewan in Canada.

- **This dinosaur** was stocky and thick-set. It grew to about 30 ft in length, and weighed about 5 tons.

- **_Triceratops_** is easily recognized by its large, frilly head shield and three large, forward-facing horns.

- **The shield** around the neck probably helped to control body temperature, as it was supplied with blood vessels.

- **The horns** may have been for defense, or to help with feeding, by pulling tree branches down toward the mouth.

DID YOU KNOW?

Like modern male deer, male Triceratops may have fought each other with their horns to secure mates.

- **With its head down** and long, sharp horns pointing forward, _Triceratops_ may have been able to fight off large predators.

- **Walking** on all four legs, it is thought that _Triceratops_ lived in herds, wandering through the Cretaceous forests.

▼ *Complete skeletons, such as this one from North America, show where the muscles and other soft tissues were attached, and allow accurate reconstructions of Triceratops.*

Compsognathus

▼ *The very delicate bone structure, teeth, and skull are well preserved in this specimen of* Compsognathus.

🔹 **Not all dinosaurs** were large. *Compsognathus* grew to only 5 ft in length. It probably weighed around 6.6 lb about the same size as a pet cat.

🔹 **Fossils of Compsognathus** have been discovered in France and Germany.

🔹 ***Compsognathus*** fossils from Germany occur in the same strata as those of the earliest bird, *Archaeopteryx*.

- *Compsognathus* lived during the late Jurassic Period, around 150 mya.

- **This dinosaur** was slender, with a very long, thin tail and a long neck.

- **The head** was large and equipped with small, sharp teeth. The large eyes would have helped it to follow fast-moving prey.

- **With long, thin legs**, *Compsognathus* would have been able to run quickly in pursuit of prey such as lizards.

- **This dinosaur** probably fed on smaller vertebrates and on invertebrates such as worms and insects, using its two sharp claws on each hand for gripping.

- *Compsognathus* lived around warm, salty lagoons, in a richly vegetated area. Limestone that formed in the lagoons contains some of the best-preserved fossils ever discovered.

DID YOU KNOW?

Because the fossils of Compsognathus and Archaeopteryx are so similar, paleontologists originally mistook some Archaeopteryx fossils for those of Compsognathus.

▶ Compsognathus *was a fierce predator of small prey such as insects, lizards, and perhaps even newly hatched dinosaurs.*

341

Allosaurus

- **Allosaurus** was a fierce, predatory dinosaur that lived in late Jurassic times about 150 mya.

- **This dinosaur** grew to around 36 ft in length, and may have weighed up to 3 tons.

- **Allosaurus** stood on its large back limbs, and used its smaller front pair for grasping prey.

- **The fingers** on the front limbs each had three long, sharp, backward-pointing claws.

- **The skull** was large but lightweight. The mouth was filled with curved, serrated teeth, ideal for tearing flesh of prey.

- **The tail** was long and tapering. This would have balanced the weight of *Allosaurus'* neck and body as it stood upright.

- **Allosaurus** fossils have mainly been found in the U.S. Some fossils also occur in southern Africa and a similar type in Victoria, Australia.

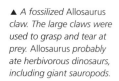

▲ *A fossilized* Allosaurus *claw. The large claws were used to grasp and tear at prey.* Allosaurus *probably ate herbivorous dinosaurs, including giant sauropods.*

- **One of the most spectacular** collections of dinosaur bones ever found was a mass of over 60 *Allosaurus* skeletons. These were discovered at the Cleveland-Lloyd Dinosaur Quarry in Utah, U.S.

🔸 **It has been suggested** that these 60 *Allosaurus* became trapped in a swamp as they attacked giant sauropods feeding there.

🔸 **Herbivorous dinosaurs** were the main prey of *Allosaurus*. The large sauropod dinosaurs such as *Diplodocus* may have lived in herds for safety.

▲ Allosaurus *had jaws that could bend slightly to allow them to open extremely wide. Together with its vicious front claws, this made* Allosaurus *a fearful predator.*

Iguanodon

🔹 **Iguanodon** was a large, herbivorous dinosaur that lived during the early part of the Cretaceous Period (135 mya).

🔹 **This dinosaur** grew to around 33 ft long, and may have weighed 4 tons.

🔹 **Iguanodon** walked on its strong hind legs, and may at times have also moved on all four limbs.

🔹 **The front limbs** were designed for grasping, with long flexible "fingers."

🔹 **Fossils** of *Iguanodon* have been found mainly in Europe, in Belgium, Germany, and Spain. The first was discovered in Sussex, U.K., in the 1820s.

🔹 **Iguanodon** was first described by Gideon Mantell, an English medical doctor and fossil collector, in 1825. His wife had earlier found the fossil teeth in a heap of stones by the road.

◀ Iguanodon's "hands" were probably good at grasping vegetation.

- **The fossil teeth** were very like those of a modern iguana. Mantell therefore named the dinosaur *Iguanodon*.

- *Iguanodon* fed on plant material, which it grasped using its hands. Its teeth, set in a beaklike snout, were for grinding vegetation.

DID YOU KNOW?

On its "hand," Iguanodon had a large thumb-spike. Early paleontologists thought this was a horn that fitted on the creature's nose.

- **More than 30** complete *Iguanodon* skeletons were discovered in a coal mine in Belgium in 1878. It seems that a herd had become trapped in a ravine and had been preserved by sand and mud.

▲ Iguanodon *walked upright, using its heavy tail to balance. It may have sometimes walked on all fours.*

Saurolophus

- *Saurolophus* belongs to a group of dinosaurs classified as the hadrosaurs. They are sometimes called duck-billed dinosaurs.

- **Hadrosaur fossils** occur mainly in North America, but some have been found in eastern Asia.

- **This group** of dinosaurs lived toward the end of the Cretaceous Period, about 80–70 mya.

- **Hadrosaurs** were large, upright-standing dinosaurs, which grew to around 40 ft in length.

- **The hind limbs** were strong, for walking, and the front limbs much smaller, for grasping plant material.

- **Plants** were chewed by the many rows of teeth in the animal's cheeks.

- **Hadrosaurs** had unusual skulls, with wide, elongated, beaklike snouts.

- **On the top** of the skull was a bony crest, which in some genera, such as *Parasaurolophus,* extended well beyond the back of the head.

- **Many suggestions** have been made by paleontologists for the function of the hadrosaur crest. It was linked to the nostrils by hollow passages, and may have been used for air storage, when the animal fed on underwater plants.

- **The hadrosaur's bony crest** may have given it a very good sense of smell. This was important for a creature that was preyed on by carnivores.

◀ The bony crest was the most distinctive feature of Parasaurolophus. Its exact function is not certain, but it was probably linked to the respiratory system, and may have been used to make sounds such as honks and bellows, perhaps at breeding time.

Tyrannosaurus

🦴 ***Tyrannosaurus*** is one of the most famous dinosaurs. Its name has become synonymous with fierce predation.

🦴 **This dinosaur** was one of the very last to evolve. It lived toward the end of the Cretaceous Period, around 70–65 mya.

🦴 **Fossils** of *Tyrannosaurus* come from Alberta and Saskatchewan, Canada, and Wyoming, Montana, and Colorado, U.S.

🦴 **The first *Tyrannosaurus* fossils** were discovered in 1902, and for many years only a few skeletons were known. In the last 40 years, many new finds have been made.

🦴 ***Tyrannosaurus*** was a giant predator, growing to more than 30 ft in length and weighing as much as 6.5 tons.

🦴 **This huge dinosaur** stood and walked on its massive hind legs. The weight of its body was balanced by its thick tail.

🦴 **It is thought that** *Tyrannosaurus* could run at around 18 mph, especially when chasing prey.

🦴 **The teeth** in its huge jaws were up to 7 in long. They had serrations, which would help tear flesh.

🦴 **The skull** had very strong muscles to provide power to the jaws. It also had flexible areas, which may have helped to cushion collisions when attacking prey.

▶ Some Tyrannosaurus *fossils show injuries that may have been caused by the teeth of another Tyrannosaurus. Perhaps they were fighting over food, territory, or breeding partners.*

Deinonychus

Although small, *Deinonychus* was one of the fiercest predators, equipped with vicious claws and teeth.

Deinonychus lived during the middle of the Cretaceous Period, about 115–105 mya.

Fossils of *Deinonychus* have been found in Montana and Wyoming, U.S.

This dinosaur grew to about 20 ft in length and weighed 130 lb.

The skeleton of *Deinonychus* reveals that it was a very active dinosaur. It would have run rapidly, and could probably leap onto large dinosaurs as it attacked them.

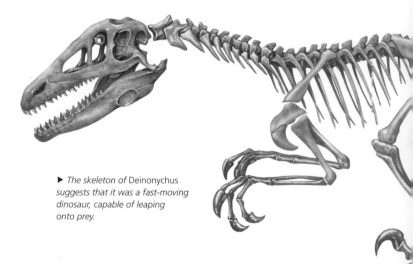

▶ The skeleton of Deinonychus suggests that it was a fast-moving dinosaur, capable of leaping onto prey.

- **The tail** was stiffened by bony tendons and strongly interlocking vertebrae.

- **The elongated head** contained rows of backward-facing, saw-edged teeth, and the hind feet had a large, sickle-shaped claw on the second toe.

- **Because it was a small dinosaur**, *Deinonychus* would have fed on small mammals, juvenile dinosaurs, and lizards.

- **A pack of *Deinonychus*** hunting together could have brought down a large dinosaur, jumping on it and slashing it with their claws. The stiff tail would help it balance during such movements.

- **It has been suggested** that *Deinonychus* was warm-blooded. Birds may have evolved from this type of dinosaur.

▼ *Packs of* Deinonychus *may have been able to outrun larger dinosaurs, bring them down and kill them for food.*

Pterodactyls

◗ **Pterodactyls belong to a group** of flying reptiles called the pterosaurs.

◗ *Pterosaurs* lived during the Triassic, Jurassic, and Cretaceous periods, at the same time as the dinosaurs.

◗ **Pterodactyls** are found fossilized in rocks of Jurassic and Cretaceous age.

◗ **The first fossil** pterosaur was discovered in southern Germany in 1784.

◗ **At first** this fossil was thought to be of an aquatic creature. Later studies found it to be of extremely light construction, and its very long fourth finger was interpreted as a wing support.

▲ Pterosaurs, like the pterodactyls, could glide but could not fly as efficiently as most birds—their wings were far less flexible.

▼ Pteranodon *was one of the later and larger pterosaurs and lived about 70 mya. It swooped over the sea to scoop up fish. Its wingspan was up to 33 ft.*

- **The name** *Pterodactylus* (wing finger) was given to this German fossil.

- **The bones** of *Pterodactylus* were hollow to minimize the creature's weight—an adaptation for flight.

- *Pterodactylus* had a long beaklike snout and claws at the front corners of its leathery wings.

- **A detailed study** of the braincases of some pterodactyl skulls shows that these creatures had large brains, which were in some respects similar to those of birds.

- *Pterodactylus* probably flew in a gliding fashion, and may have swooped down to catch prey.

Diplodocus

- *Diplodocus* was a giant herbivore, and it lived at the end of the Jurassic Period, around 150 mya.

- **Weighing** around 10–20 tons, *Diplodocus* was one of the lighter large quadrupeds. It was, however, the longest of this type of dinosaur, being 88.5 ft in length.

- **Diplodocid fossils** have been found in North America, especially in Colorado and Wyoming, U.S.

- **With a large body** to support, *Diplodocus* stood on four massive legs. These had hooflike claws, apart from the three inner toes, which had sharper, longer claws.

- **The thick legs** acted like the supports on a suspension bridge, with its backbone in the same position as the roadway between them.

- **The neck** and tail were very long. The tail tapered gradually, and had a whiplike end.

- **A modern** interpretation of the animal's body suggests that the tail did not drag on the ground, as had been previously thought. It was almost certainly held well off the ground.

DID YOU KNOW?

Diplodocus's nostrils were so high up on its skull that experts once thought it had a trunk like an elephant's.

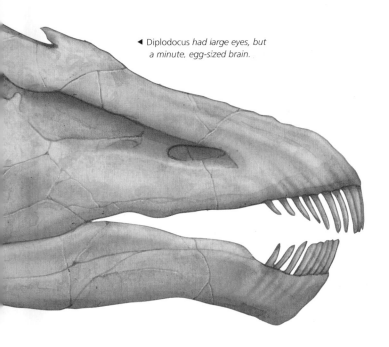

◀ Diplodocus *had large eyes, but a minute, egg-sized brain.*

🔹 **The skull** of *Diplodocus* had large eye sockets, and nostrils positioned high above the jaws, which had thin teeth set right at the front. The braincase was tiny, about the size of a hen's egg.

🔹 **Like other giant sauropods**, *Diplodocus* was a herbivore. The teeth did no more than tear off leaves. In the stomach these were broken up by gastroliths (swallowed stones).

Archaeopteryx

In 1861, the fossil of an unknown creature that seemed to have the impressions of feathers was discovered at Solnhofen in southern Germany.

The fossils from Solnhofen are called *Archaeopteryx*, which means "ancient wing."

This has proved to be one of the most important fossils, as it is the earliest known bird.

The late Jurassic limestone at Solnhofen is famous for its detailed preservation of very delicate organisms.

Archaeopteryx has many features similar to those of small dinosaurs. Its jaws, for example, have rows of small teeth.

▲ With a covering of feathers, Archaeopteryx is one of the earliest birdlike creatures in the fossil record.

- **The reptilian tail** is also long and bony, and there are claws on its wing-supporting arms.

- **The presence of feathers**, and the large eyes and brain, are all true bird features.

- **The bones** in the *Archaeopteryx* skeleton are not as lightweight as those of modern birds.

- **It is probable** that *Archaeopteryx* could glide rather than fly efficiently.

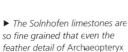

▶ *The Solnhofen limestones are so fine grained that even the feather detail of* Archaeopteryx *is preserved.*

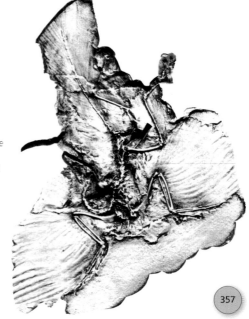

The first mammals

🔺 **Mammals** differ from reptiles in a number of important ways. They have fur, are warm-blooded, and feed their young with milk. Also, the great majority of mammals give birth to live young.

🔺 **The first mammals** are found fossilized in rocks from the Triassic Period (248–206 mya).

🔺 **Near Bristol, U.K.,** is a famous site for early mammal fossils. Here, deposits containing mammal remains from a Triassic cave floor were washed into a crack in the underlying Carboniferous limestone.

🔺 **The early mammals** that lived at the same time as dinosaurs may have been at least partly nocturnal. Their skulls have large eye sockets, suggesting good vision.

🔺 **In Jurassic rock** in South Africa are the remains of *Megazostrodon*, one of the best-documented early mammals.

- *Megazostrodon* had a shrewlike body and a long snout filled with sharp teeth.

- **It is thought that** *Megazostrodon* hunted at night for invertebrate prey such as insects.

- **Another early mammal** was *Morganucodon*. This rodentlike creature had very large eye sockets in its tiny skull, and may also have been nocturnal.

▲ Leptictidium *combined the features of a weasel, a shrew, and a kangaroo! Like other small carnivores, it probably hunted at night.*

- **The braincase** suggests good hearing as well as good vision. Paleontologists studying the jaws of *Morganucodon* believe that, like some modern mammals, it may have had two sets of teeth during its life, and was possibly fed on milk when very young.

359

Megatherium

▶ Megatherium *used its considerable height to feed from trees. Few other mammals could compete with this feeding strategy.*

- **After their development** through the Mesozoic Era, many giant forms of mammals evolved in the Cenozoic.

- **Tree sloths** evolved during the Eocene Epoch (56–34 mya).

- *Megatherium* was a close relation to the sloths and grew to more than 19 ft tall. It first appeared about 6 mya.

DID YOU KNOW?

Large quantities of Megatherium dung are common in some caves in Argentina. One such deposit caught fire and burned for six months!

- **Fossil remains** of *Megatherium* have been found in both North and South America, mainly from cave deposits.

- **Much is known** about *Megatherium*, as it only became extinct around 12,000 years ago.

- **As well as bones**, some soft tissue and hair have been found.

- **There are stories** in Argentina that these giant sloths only died out a few hundred years ago, hunted by humans.

- *Megatherium* had a thick tail and massive hind legs to support it when it stood upright.

- **The snout** was extended forward and it had no front teeth. The animal probably grasped tree branches with its strong front limbs and pulled off the leaves.

Paraceratherium

- **Fossilized remains** of *Paraceratherium* (formerly known as either *Baluchitherium* or *Indricotherium*) have been found in Asia and Europe.

- *Paraceratherium* is classified as a perissodactyl.

- **These mammals** are characterized by having odd numbers of toes on their hoofs. Animals with hoofs are called ungulates.

- **Only about 19 or 20 species** of perissodactyls live today. Their even-toed ungulate cousins, the artiodactyls, have between 220–230 species living today.

- **Paraceratherium** lived during the Oligocene Epoch (34–23 mya).

- **This mammal** was a giant, hornless rhinoceros, with a long neck, and massive legs that supported its huge body.

- **The head** of *Paraceratherium* was relatively small, and in the males, slightly dome-shaped.

- **Reaching** 17.8 ft in height at its shoulder, *Paraceratherium* was the largest-known land mammal ever.

- **This enormous mammal** could easily reach the tops of quite tall trees to browse on leaves.

DID YOU KNOW?

At 20 tons, Paraceratherium weighed as much as four large elephants. It may have lived in small groups like modern rhinoceroses.

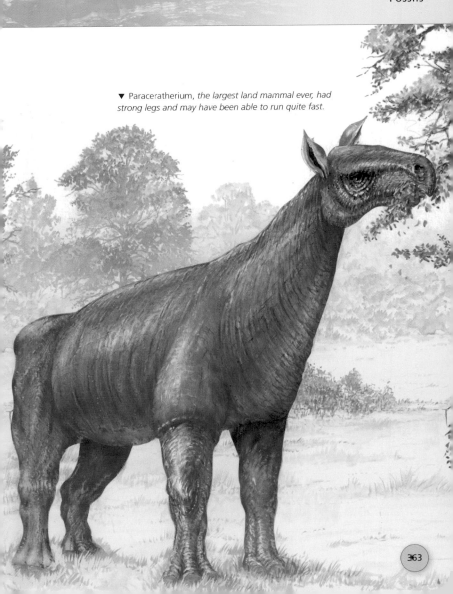

▼ Paraceratherium, *the largest land mammal ever, had strong legs and may have been able to run quite fast.*

Giant whales

🐚 **Mammals** took to the sea early during the Eocene Epoch, about 50 mya.

🐚 **Most marine mammals** belong to the biological order Cetacea, which includes the whales, dolphins, and porpoises.

🐚 **One of the oldest fossil whales,** *Pakicetus,* comes from Eocene rocks in Pakistan.

🐚 **Fossils** of the giant Eocene whale, *Basilosaurus,* were first discovered in the 1830s.

🐚 ***Basilosaurus*** grew to more than 66 ft in length. Its body was slim, and the head, with rows of large triangular teeth, was rather small. Modern whales have large heads.

🐚 **Instead of a blowhole** like modern whales, *Basilosaurus* had nostrils.

- **The body** would have been able to flex in the water to provide power for swimming and the broad front flippers acted as rudders.

- **The rear limbs** were virtually nonexistent. They were simply small bony structures within the body.

- **In 1990**, new fossils of *Basilosaurus* were found, which showed that the insignificant internal rear limbs had all the bones of fully formed legs.

- **The largest-known animal** to have ever lived, the modern blue whale, grows up to 100 ft in length.

▲ The prehistoric whale Basilosaurus, *which means "king of the lizards," was so named because the first person to examine its remains thought it was a gigantic plesiosaur—a prehistoric marine reptile.*

Ice Age monsters

◀ **The last** great Ice Age began around 2 mya. There have been some dramatic climatic changes during this time.

◀ **Some mammals** grew to a great size during the Ice Age. Perhaps the best known is the woolly mammoth.

◀ **A fully grown** adult mammoth stood 9 ft tall at the shoulder.

◀ **The mammoth's skin** was well insulated, with a thick coat of hair.

▼ *Woolly mammoths 1, musk ox 2 and giant elk 3 wander across the frozen tundra in search of vegetation to feed on.*

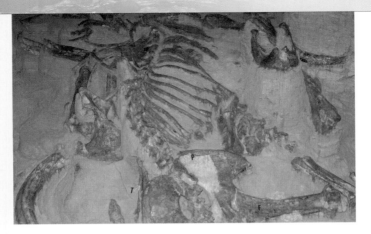

▲ *This mass of mammoth bones, including an almost complete set of ribs, is from Siberia, where it was found in frozen earth.*

One function of the mammoth's huge tusks may have been to sweep snow away from the tundra vegetation on which it fed.

The remains of mammoths have been found in Europe, Asia, and North America.

Many tons of tusks and bones of woolly mammoths have been found.

Finds of mammoth tusks have, in the past, been plundered for their ivory.

Our human ancestors would have hunted mammoths for food. These elephants only became extinct about 10,000 years ago.

Hominid fossils

Hominids are mammals that belong to our "human" group. These creatures are different from apes and other primates because most probably walked upright on their hind legs.

There are many different hominid fossils from various parts of the world, and it is not easy to work out a complete family tree.

The earliest hominid fossils may be of a creature called *Ardipithecus* from Ethiopia.

An important group of early hominids are the Australopithicenes. These upright-walking creatures lived in east and southern Africa between 3.5 and 2 mya.

Working in Chad, in central Africa, a team of French paleontologists found a hominidlike skull in 2002, which may be seven million years old. This may be a link between apes and hominids.

The earliest fossils belonging to our genus, *Homo*, are the remains of *Homo habilis* from the world-famous Olduvai Gorge in Tanzania.

Many other species of *Homo* have been discovered. Around 2 mya, *Homo ergaster* lived in Kenya, Africa.

Homo erectus lived at the same time as *Homo ergaster* but in Europe and Asia. It became extinct only 50,000 years ago. *Homo erectus* could use fire.

Our own species, *Homo sapiens*, began less than 200,000 years ago in Africa. Fossils trace its spread around the world.

▼ *This skull of* Homo habilis *is flattened without a forehead. Its braincase is much smaller than ours.*

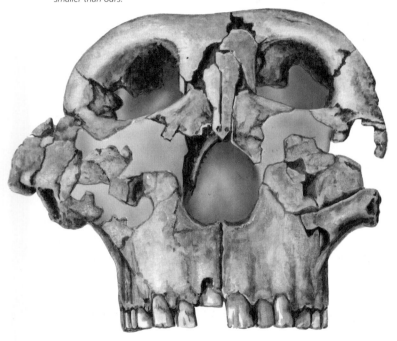

Fossils of *Homo neanderthalensis* have been found in many parts of Europe and Asia. These hominids were highly organized, and died out around 29,000 years ago.

Index

Index

Entries in **bold** refer to main subject entries; entries in *italics* refer to illustrations.

Acknowledgments

All artwork from the Miles Kelly Artwork Bank

The publishers would like to thank the following sources
for the use of their photographs:

Front cover Richard Becker/FLPA

Back cover (t) Fotolia.com, (c) Vuk Varuna/Shutterstock.com,
(b) Joe Gough/Shutterstock.com

Dreamstime
17 Bdingman; 64 Bob621; 192 Kyolshin; 222 Jonnightin; 250 Gaja

Fotolia.com
34 Alexwhite; 35 Pshenichka; 56 Albo; 69 BANNER; 139 chinellatophoto;
153 chezbriand;160 Cornelius; 164 J.+W Roth

iStockphoto.com
26 desy_sevdanova; 50 Froggery; 55 ImagineGolf; 80 Abuelo Ramiro; 99 lissart;
182 lissart; 217 Maxfocus

All other photographs courtesy of Chris and Helen Pellent

Every effort has been made to acknowledge the
source and copyright holder of each picture.
Miles Kelly Publishing apologizes for any
unintentional errors or omissions.